STONE
PALACES

STONE
PALACES

THE MOUNTAINEERS BOOKS

GEOF CHILDS

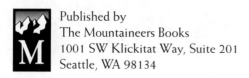
Published by
The Mountaineers Books
1001 SW Klickitat Way, Suite 201
Seattle, WA 98134

First hardcover printing: 2000
First paper printing: 2001

Published simultaneously in Great Britain by Cordee, 3a DeMontfort Street, Leicester, England, LE1 7HD

Manufactured in the United States of America

Managing Editor: Kathleen Cubley
Copyeditor: Uma Kukathas
Book and cover design by Pam Hidaka

Cover photographs: *Snow Creek Wall* by Sean Courage, *Vesper Peak's North Face* by Jim Nelson.

Interior photographs: *Supercrack Buttress* by Gregg Adams, *Mount Phunghi, Himalaya, Nepal* by Pat Morrow, *Southern Utah* by Gregg Adams, *Early Winters Peak* by Jim Nelson, *Ice Axes* by Gregg Adams.

Library of Congress Cataloging-in-Publication Data
Childs, Geoffrey, 1946–
    Stone palaces / by Geoffrey Childs.—1st ed.
        p.   cm.
    Includes index,
    ISBN 0-89886-732-0 (hardcover)
    1. Mountaineering. I. Title.
    GV199.83 .C46 2000
    796.52'2—dc21   00-008895

I cannot say that all of this is not strange ...

—Masha Lipman, *The New Yorker*

—W. H. Auden, *Collected Poems*

TABLE OF CONTENTS

INTRODUCTION

Memories. You're talking about memories.

—Harrison Ford, *Blade Runner*

～～

valley. In one direction, the valley traces the contour of the
and in the other it pursues vanished sheets of ice. Beyond the western
curve of the range, rain clouds dull the far horizon. Dust storms billow
to the east. In all directions glaciers, waterfalls, and shining slabs of rock
spackle the flanks of a thousand hillsides. It is an astonishing place to sit
and meditate on the felicity of nature. But what brings me here is at my
feet. Fifteen hundred feet below me is the canyon I call home.

If I have remembered to bring binoculars I can just make out the
roof of our house. It sits on a conifer bench facing south across a plain of
knapweed and wild alfalfa. Five miles to the north our downtown commercial district resides at the intersection of seldom-used roads. No more
than two stores and a guide service, it has no street corners, crack houses,
or civic officials. It's the kind of community in which the best-known
citizens are over seventy, under seven, or dogs. Where rummage sales
and potluck dinners constitute the only form of government, and where
latte-sipping carpenters raise kids who know more about waxing skis
than they do about baseball. Where sunset, like a point of view, takes
hours in the unraveling.

Despite—or perhaps because of—these assets, the Valley is a hard
place to wrest a living from. For generations people have come here in
the hope of earning a minimalist's wages off the land, only to have their
dreams collapse beneath the weight of economic reality. Yet even as the

failed ranches and forgotten mining claims of the last wave make room for million-dollar vacation homes, the dream survives among the local proletariat, though these days pursuit of the good life weighs less heavily upon driving cows and cutting trees than on recreation. With skiing, running, biking, fishing, paddling, and climbing present in abundance, a bustling subeconomy of builders, realtors, guides, and shop owners has evolved to meet the needs of a growing contingent of weekend athletes. A short tour up any side road quickly reveals the area's outdoor bias—luxury SUVs and decrepit trucks alike sit outside garages where mountain bikes, skis, kayaks, and climbing gear occupy the most valued shelter. A province of surprising wealth and deceptive poverty, it is the last best place in America and about as close to paradise as I am ever likely to get.

Getting here has been a project. It's tempting to say that the ride has been worth all the wrong turns, but sometimes I'm not so sure. Maybe if I had been operating on a plan more driven by reason than luck I could take greater satisfaction in my journey, but the fact is that for most of my life I have operated on a plan more resembling the junk drawer on my work bench than the digital logic on my wrist. Not that I feel anything less than inordinately lucky, mind you. After all, somewhere in between being born in Detroit and settling down in Mazama I have lived in Paris, wintered in Maine, summered in Manhattan, survived a happy childhood, and driven a taxi, truck, motorcycle, and more nails than I care to remember. I've been to art school. I have served in the military, spent the weekend in jail, written a book, and studied at an Ivy League school. I have worked in factories, forests, education, and industry; played hockey, fired a hand gun, ridden a snowboard (skipped the tattoos), and learned a little something from most of my worst mistakes. I have taken life and brought life into the world. I have climbed peaks unclimbed by anyone else and skied snow unserved by machinery other than my own slow approach. I have heard the silent thunder of my own heart and the roar at the end of everything. I have been terribly afraid and terribly happy, cold to the core and warm as a peanut. I have been rich and poor, overfed and undernourished. I have ducked at all the right times, avoided most of the worse forms of dental surgery, and never experienced chronic back pain. I have good knees. I have been to the Louvre.

But, you might ask—and you would be justified in doing so—So what? So what, indeed! Other than an enviable address, what has it all amounted to? At an age when most of my peers are beginning to think

tend to you would think we would behave more prudently do things we can't afford with money we don't have simply because we can't *not* do them. While more sensible acquaintances have ridden the stock market to comfortable wealth, we have squandered our savings on expeditions and adventures as if somehow playing was more important than having had our noses pressed to the grindstone...or, more realistically, the nether regions of some supercilious corporate official.

A friend of mine used to say that a good adventure has the same components as a good life: high endeavor, questionable outcome, and good companionship. I think he might be right. Life, at its richest, should be an adventure. An experience. A corner turned. Moments of doubt in the company of good friends en route to someplace, something, or someone that matters. So if our investment strategy has been a bust, at least we can hope that the adventure of living while we had the chance is inheritance enough for our son.

For most of my adult life mountains have provided that mix of suspense, desire, and friendship. In fact, just about everything worthwhile I have gotten out of this world has somehow been connected to mountains. I met my wife and almost all of my best friends through climbing. I have looked deepest and seen the furthest from the sides of high peaks. And despite what it may have cost in terms of financial well-being, my affair with the world's high places has left me a wealth of memories which, examined, teem with the frozen grins of friends both living and dead in the healthiest, happiest, most satisfying moments of our lives. If once more given the choice between the hills or Harvard I would take the mountains every time. They have treated me fairer and introduced me to a better class of people than any career ever could have.

I would not argue that it has been a choice that has been easy for my family or those close to me. How do you explain obsessive love to someone who does not share your passion? How do you rationalize the contradictions of climbing: its brilliant triviality and sublime uselessness, its beauty and hardship? Or more significantly, how in these days of record-breaking financial expansion do you justify the anti-capitalist notion of putting your life at risk to achieve something so difficult, so utterly and completely demanding...and then just turning around and walking away from it? The answer is that you can't, of course. There is no common sense to it. It is a lousy way to get rich and a very imperfect path to enlightenment. Yet the older I get the more clear it becomes to me that if in the end all that remains to us are our memories, then among the misfired synapses and disorderly recollections of my old age will be the faces, places, and adventures of a life well spent. And that, I think, will be quite enough.

~~

It has been said that in medieval times certain scholars were able to erect "memory palaces" from the details, people, places, and events of their lives. Practitioners of this art were then able to roam the hallways of these imaginary castles at will, stopping by specific rooms to revisit in exquisite detail such memories as they cared to revive. The most skilled, it has been written, were able to recall select events even decades after they occurred with the same facility that you or I might "fetch an old coat from a trunk in the attic."[1]

This book is my palace. Only this palace has been constructed of stone. Erected from the people, places, events, emotions, and imaginings of nearly a quarter of a century of climbing and life in the mountains.

Unlike my medieval predecessors I do not vouch for the accuracy of my memories. Walk through these doors and you enter into a kingdom where the distinction between truth and fiction, now and then, who and what, matters less than the telling of the tale. In my halls, fact and fantasy combine to entertain, not to educate.

and of the people who go there, the things they say and do, and things they wish they hadn't. Exactly the way in which all the best climbing stories have always been told. Anyway, I hope you enjoy them.

---

[1]"Memory Building," The Economist (September 4, 1998), p.70.

PART I
Routes and Passages

THE COLD SEASON

[Climbing] is the chance to be briefly free of the small concerns of our ordinary lives, to strip off the nonessentials: these plus faith and purpose, is concentrated on the single job at hand with an unrelenting determination.

—Charles Houston, 1953 K2 Expedition

I am standing at the base of a boulder in a pine wood. On a Tuesday. At 2:55 P.M. The air is scented with benzoin, vanilla, and dust. Blood trickles down the inside of my right index finger. A translucent blob of superglue holds a damaged cuticle in place. My toes are killing me.

I take a drink of water, breathe deeply, and raise my eyes to the rock. For a moment I try to imagine the moves. My hands flutter like birds. I place the inside of my left foot on a slanting blade of granite; the tip of one finger crimps a nickel-sized edge. As my right foot leaves the ground my opposite hand wiggles into a shallow crack. Two more moves bring me to a featureless overlap. I hesitate between desire and doubt. At an age when most of my high school classmates are approaching the pinnacle of their working lives the fact that I am approaching not much more than the pinnacle of this 20-foot block of limestone flashes through my mind. Another breath to gather my composure, then I raise my heel to a ledge. A long reach, a moment's acceleration, and suddenly I am on top. Shadows flicker across the rock. The pines hiss like serpents and, to the best of my knowledge, the world is neither better nor worse for my boldness.

It is a silly thing to do at fifty-two. Maturity is supposed to have made a spectator of me by now. But I am still hungry. Still studying the hillsides around my home in search of undiscovered stone. The conversations that occupy my greatest interest have nothing to do with hedge funds or 401ks. They are about the arcane details of crack width and fixed gear. The important decisions in my life are not made over the phone or in an office. They are made at the long end of an 11-millimeter rope. A place where time and temptation form a perfect meritocracy in which all victories are temporary and all failure forgiven.

It would be less than truthful to call this place paradise. Climbing

amounted to anything more than money. Money that brought me back here, back to the beginning. Back to this boulder—feet squashed into shoes so tight they have deformed my gait, fingertips cross-hatched with the geology of a life measured better by moves than market forces.

So, at late middle age I am without savings, without insurance, and without much in the way of college tuition for my son. Plans for big walls and distant ranges dispel any regret. There is no looking back. What has passed is past; there are always more mountains. I work as a guide. My wife works in a shop. On the side I sell climbing gear, write articles, and do whatever else it takes to maintain a positive cash flow. She teaches skiing. We split cooking and childcare. Love and laughter we get for free. As Eric Beck once noted, "At either end of the social spectrum there lies a leisure class."

We live among friends. There are only about 120 of us at this end of the valley, so people look out for each other. It is 14 miles to the nearest town, 22 miles to the nearest medical care, 60 miles to the only traffic light in the county. There are glaciers closer than that: a million acres of wild America howling outside a door that we have never once locked. In the summer we drag an old bed frame outside and sleep under a sky as ink black and open as it must have been when the first human being came to these hills blinking with the sheer joy of its perfection. These are the happiest days of our lives.

I recognize that the future will change all this in ways that I cannot predict. I already feel my skills beginning to diminish, the strength ebbing from my arms. That's okay. The rules of the game are both flexible and just. In climbing you get only what you deserve. When I look at the vicissitudes of the workplace—the politics, downsizing, and second-guessing that so beleaguer my friends—it seems far more cruel. A former colleague once whispered to me, "I am not alive in this office." In fact, he was not. With two mortgages, three car payments, half a dozen other loans, and a credit card statement that fills four pages of fine print, the parameters of his world had shrunk to the scale of his boss. If you ask me, the most jumbled Himalayan icefall is an oasis of justice and stability in comparison.

⌐⌐

It is after 4 P.M. when I change shoes and start down to where I left my pack. Unseen mountains throw their shadow over the valley. A Stellar's jay chirps from the branches of a ponderosa. Dead leaves crack like glass beneath my feet.

I cross a dry creek bed and depart Forest Service land. This is private property. The boundaries are important. I go more carefully here.

It is that way with climbing, too. Since style and ethics are a function of personal responsibility, the way in which one climbs tells much about him. Who he is and what he values is written in the rock. Indeed, the very act of dropping a rope over my shoulder places limits on my behavior far more stringent than those imposed by society. Though it is no more the sum of me than my teeth, I would be less than what I am without climbing, less for having missed out on what Walter Lipman calls "the useless, the brave, noble, divinely foolish, and very wisest things that are done by man."

Back at the truck I stop and gaze up at Goat Wall. The weather is turning. In a few weeks ice will begin to form in its gullies. An involuntary shiver runs through me. The cold season lies just ahead. I know the terrain: the days of self-doubt, the roaring nights, and profound aloneness. I go to it laughing. It is the easiest thing I have ever done.

CHALK

We have only one person to blame, and that's each other.

—Larry Beck, New York Rangers (on the reason for a fight)

There are few things that are harder to sympathize with than the moral broodings of a generation past. Chlorinated water and trade unionism, for example, hardly strike us as major issues anymore. But there was a time when people were happily willing to shoot holes in each other over the right to whiter teeth and fair wages. In climbing, the parallels are many. Gymnastic chalk and the machine driven bolt are two.

It was not that long ago that the bolts that have now become a feature at almost every crag in North America were a source of widespread controversy. Reputations were ruined and routes vandalized by zealots on both sides of the issue. So fresh are the wounds left by bolting that it is easy to forget there was a time when chalk was a topic of almost equal gravity and concern.

I was living on Mount Desert Island, Maine, the first time I ever used chalk, and I remember the circumstances well. The surf-washed cliffs and roadside crags of Acadia National Park, at the island's center, were largely unknown outside of Maine in those days, a circumstance that left its sea stacks, splitter cracks, and untraveled faces largely in the hands of us locals. We knew this happy idyll could not last forever, and by the summer of 1975 the pressure from outsiders was already beginning to mount. Climbers from Boston, North Conway, and Connecticut were showing up in greater numbers than ever. Determined to grab as many lines for myself as possible, I was enjoying a particularly energetic season when the weather went bad. Bad as in hot. And hot in the way that only coastal New England can be hot. Week after week with temperatures in the high nineties, the sky cloudless, and the zephyrs that dragged themselves in off the North Atlantic so sodden with humidity that with every move you made it felt as if you were lifting the whole weight of the sky. Our bodies shone with sweat, our feet baked through the black soles of our EBs, and lichen fell from the walls like spindrift. It was enough

somely embroidered bags carried at their waists. Though I knew the practice to be controversial I was struck by its practicality. Clearly, chalk offered a significant advantage in dealing with the humidity of the human hand—exactly the characteristic I had in mind when I entered a local drug store and asked if they had any. The druggist eyed me quizzically and then found a single block on the bottom of a long-forgotten shelf. He charged me 25 cents for it and told me that, to the best of his knowledge, it was a laxative for babies.

Back in my apartment I unwrapped the block and examined it closely. Its appearance was inoffensive, deceptive, clean. I ran my hand over the surface of the cube and rubbed my fingertips together. The sudden stickiness of my grip was both stunning and unsettling. Surely, I thought to myself, no one who is less than a 5.11 leader has any justification for using this magical substance. But then, massaging the block and placing my hand against the wall, I quivered at the thought of clinging upside down to a wall of tenuous friction. It was with this image in mind that I replaced the block in its bag and shoved it to the far corner of a drawer.

Less than a week later Steve Shea, an Aspen climber, and I were trying to free a short, poorly protected aid route when he pulled a chalk bag out of his pocket, dipped, and then danced where I later struggled hopelessly to follow. Returning home I immediately transferred the chalk from the back of my drawer to the bottom of a small stuff sack. Then, for practice, I clipped the string through the snap on the front of my shorts and, stemming between the baseboards in one corner of the living room, carefully bouldered to the bathroom and back stopping every few feet to dip my fingers into the bag. The rush of power that coursed through my body obliterated any moral concerns. In a flash of light I suddenly realized that all that had ever stood between me and raising my standard was chalk! Stepping down, I placed the stuff sack with my climbing gear, opened a can of beer, and solemnly vowed never to use it on anything less than 5.10...or maybe hard 5.9—unless, of course, I was really, really scared or feeling kind of off-form or something like that, in which case I could probably use it down to, oh, say 5.6 or something.

Without a doubt the transcendent event in Eastern rock climbing that summer had been Sam Streibert's and Bob Anderson's freeing of the VMC route on Cannon Cliff. Having done the route on aid, this achievement struck me as more impressive than days two, four, and five of Creation and, frankly, not that far behind the advent of fire. So when the phone rang and I heard Sam on the other end of the line asking if I wanted to go climbing, it was as if divine convergence had settled any qualms I might have had about the use of chalk. I knew immediately what route we should do: an obscure corner hung well up on the side of a cliff called the South Bubbles. I told Sam about the route and explained to him that it didn't look that hard—maybe 5.9 or easy 5.10. I also told him that it got sun in the late afternoon and that we might find it a little "sweaty." Sam immediately agreed to an attempt, and we made plans to meet the next day.

As I hung up the phone my mind did cartwheels. A vision of Sam—trembling at his belay stance, hands held together in prayer as I pulled through the crux—formed in my imagination. The climb was a setup, of course. It would be scorching hot up there and Sam, I knew, did not use chalk. Slave to the myths and rituals of another generation, he wouldn't have a chance. It was with more than a certain sadness that I tucked the bag inside the top flap of my pack and opened another bottle of beer.

The next day as Sam uncoiled the rope I snapped my chalk bag into place above the zipper of my climbing shorts. Then, seizing the host's initiative, I shoved the sack in my front pocket and took the lead, quickly scrambling the initial problems with a bulge in my trousers that must

better holds and solid gear. Shifting my feet and searching for something to get my hands on, I came to the realization that, as in all climbing stories, I had reached the point where to proceed meant there would be no option of retreat.

Carefully adjusting my weight, I began to explore the smear I'd have to stand on in order to launch myself toward the crack. After several moments of moving back and forth I at last felt confidence enough in these holds to release a hand. As I reached down and pulled the stuff sack out of my pocket, I quickly stole a glance at Sam. Thank God, he was looking at the view. Then, as rehearsed, I opened the bag, fluttered my fingers inside its depths, and withdrew them. I switched hands and whitened the other. The increased tackiness of my grip was subtle—but satisfying. By this time, however, the hand I had originally dunked was utterly pumped and in need of a second trip to the chalk bag.

What followed was a drama of diminishing returns. Each time I chalked one hand the other would become increasingly fatigued and in need of re-chalking. This was obviously not a situation that could go on indefinitely. As my level of exhaustion increased so did my level of alarm. Now, instead of gently massaging the block, I was thrashing at it, whipping my hand back and forth with a vigor that sent small puffs of carbonate into the air and filled my nostrils with dust. Sweat dripped into my eyes. My feet began to tremble. Sensing that it was clearly time to move on, I thrust my hand back into the bag, shook it energetically, and had just begun to withdraw it when I felt the gentle, indescribably awful pressure of the stuff sack closing around my wrist.

Good Lord!

Trapped! I looked down in horror. The throat of that sphinctered sack had clasped my hand, sheathing it completely in nylon and leaving me feeling very much like that portion of the human anatomy that it most resembled. Using my hips to hide my struggles from Sam I immediately began pulling the sack up and down against my swami harness. I can only imagine what he must have thought I was doing! Yet the thing still refused to budge. With a growing sense of anxiety I began pawing more aggressively at the bag, flinging my hand left and right, yanking and torquing my wrist, spinning my arm in circles. None of which seemed to help in the least. Finally resorting to brute force, I jerked back on the bag sharply. There was a muted "pop" and my hand came away free though still shrouded in the upturned chalk bag. Unfortunately in liberating my hand I had snapped the button off my shorts which now, unrestrained, began a southward journey in the direction of my ankles. A long leader fall and the possibility of death suddenly paled at the thought of *being found that way!* Quickly, I threw my knees apart and squatted—a maneuver that stopped my shorts from falling any further but left me in the posture of a sumo wrestler purging himself of raw fish.

Frankly, I didn't care. Dignity was no longer of any concern to me. Whatever small flame of self-esteem still burned in my breast was rapidly suffocating in the billowing smog of magnesium carbonate that formed around me as I began frantically whipping my arm back and forth in an attempt to throw off the bag. From below, I must have appeared like the prophet Elijah ascending through a layer of strato-cumuli into heaven. In fact, so impressive was this display that several cars pulled over to the side of the road and I could hear people shouting, "Up there! Look up there!" Blinded and choking, I decided to risk one final gambit. Reinserting my hand into the pocket of my shorts, and distending my stomach, I trapped the sack between gut and thigh, and then, with a loud scream, yanked backward.

The applause and exclamations that came from the road following this maneuver were recounted to me later by Sam. So great was the cloud of particulates that erupted from the sack, he explained, that the entire lower portion of the cliff was thrown into shadow. Seventy feet above him, the sight of my now naked fingers appearing through the haze very

mediate moves. Sam, watching all this from his belay stance, must have thought that I had aged fifty years during my spell at the sharp end. Like some geriatric Icarus, my face, hair, arms, legs, and clothing had all turned completely white. My voice, as I called to him for a tightrope, was tremulous and weak. Once I reached the bottom of the difficulties I found an alternative route to the top and hastily established a belay.

Sam came up the crack. He assured me that it was hard. At least 5.10, he said, though I knew he was being generous. And to tell the truth, I have never been back to confirm his rating. In fact, I left Maine shortly after our climb and now live on the opposite side of the continent. I have never seen Sam again; never been back to the South Bubble. I do still climb. And, like everybody else, I carry a chalk bag. It's different now, though. Nobody cares about a little white powder on the rock. Besides, winters are hard here and the muck that collects on our local classics is almost always gone by spring. The residue that clings to the overhangs goes undiscussed. With so much rock to climb it seems like a small thing. The same with bolts. People come into the sport with different expectations and different desires these days. So, slave to the myths and rituals of another generation, I hold my silence and my chalk bag tight.

CHAIN GANG

First we feel. Then we fall.

—James Joyce, *Finnegans Wake*

⁓

Even at night the dam is visible from almost 30 miles away. Kleg lights illuminate its concrete walls. Red warning beacons dot the hillsides. Beneath a lattice of high-tension wires, acres of empty parking lot pave the bluff as if in anticipation of some great event. On either side of the water course parks decorate the shoreline. Only a solitary Winnebago has occupied the site closest to the restrooms. Far below, the river runs flat and silent between manicured shores. All that remains of its once wild heart and inundated geography is an occasional swirl of current. America, it has been said, is where you find it missing.

South of the dam the road switches shores. A succession of small towns flickers past and fades to black. At 3 A.M. the only entertainment my radio provides is "Pastor Bob's Old Fashioned Gospel Hour." Halfway between East Wenatchee and a good night's sleep I listen intently. Tonight the good reverend is sending a special appeal to all the somnolent Bubbas out there tripping on reds and driving eighteen-wheelers toward Seattle loaded with apples, lumber, pigs, and potatoes; an exhortation aimed at separating them from their sins and beseeching them to take out their credit cards in the service of God, the Gospel, and that long-suffering, impecunious, divinely inspired Son of the South—Pastor Bob, him self. After all, he intones, fighting iniquity is not an inexpensive enterprise.

Thick-headed with fatigue I pull in at the next convenience store. I find the sixteen-year-old night clerk sound asleep on the counter. His gray-green arm extends toward me, palm up like the limb of some emaciated tree. I fill my cup with coffee and lay a $10 bill in his hand. Outside a couple of Mexicans have pulled alongside the service island where my truck is parked. They have raised the hood of their 1962 Ford pickup and, carefully avoiding eye contact, we begin fueling our separate vehicles. Somewhere out among the dales a dog yelps and the wind ruffles

exhaust. An hour later and 5 miles south of Wherever, I turn onto a dirt road and bounce through the frozen ruts of a broken promise.

In the beginning, this place was going to be our own private Disneyworld. A mile of perfect rock and unbroken vistas. We all agreed to keep quiet about it, to park our cars where they couldn't be seen, and to cover our hiking trails with tumbleweed. It still didn't take long for word to get out. Then week after week new cars began to appear, bringing new people and new problems. The trails eroded. Piles of shit appeared under every rock. Cigarette butts littered the ground. People brought their dogs. A guidebook came out. The competition that once pushed standards and opened new opportunities eventually led to vandalism, fist fights, controversy, and lies. The government got involved. The magic disappeared.

Eventually, a few of us decided we either had to go away or change the endgame. Being selfish we decided to do both. That was how we discovered the Amphitheater. Migrating west on mountain bikes and guesswork we found the paradise we had always sought less than 2 miles from where our search had begun. A U-shaped enclosure with two caves and a spring that ran from March until late July; 90-foot-high basalt walls with rock as hard and clean as diamonds. Even now, holding the steering wheel with both hands, I can feel the texture of its stone, sense its contours, and imagine my weight pressed against its sculpted angles.

A leg up here, fingers just so. God, you'd think I could do this dance in my sleep by now, yet completion still confounds me. The pieces are still the pieces of an unfinished whole. An enigma. A treasure to unlock, a story to be told. After nearly three decades of postmodern pioneering, it is this one place that has most come to define me and my climbing. In the end, I have exhausted far fewer of its possibilities than it has of mine.

At the bottom of a long S-turn I pass the parking lot for the main area and continue along a rough path that skirts the back of an old orchard. A couple of cairns and the remains of a barbed-wire fence are all that mark the way. My truck groans for every frost heave and dried-out arroyo I cross. Coffee spills down the front of my shirt, and a piece of toast curled like paper on the seat beside me flips onto the floor. A full moon and an open sky reward my ambitions. You see, I have come here with two projects in mind. The first is a climb. A crack that compresses from hand-sized to barely the width of a fingertip, then evaporates altogether in 30 feet of pumpy face climbing. Very sweet. The other is an act of terrorism. Erasing it all. Returning it to wilderness. Letting the river run wild.

I have thought of almost nothing else for weeks. I can mime the moves of my climb as if Martha Graham had choreographed them for me. Thumbs down, thumbs up, bone and tips twice then stretch right, push away, flag to a drop-knee, dyno, dyno, hang; undercling, heel hook, match and press, match and press, side pull, switch feet, dyno, dyno, hang. With twenty-eight hours of sunlight, a Bosche humming on overload in my backpack, a milk crate full of $^5/_8$-inch Rawl drive bolts that jingle every time I hit a pothole, a hammer, some tubes of Epoxy, a 48-inch crowbar and a cold chisel, I have come here armed both to install my route and to erase it. A lot of effort, some might say, to win a game, make a point, set a standard, kill some time, stretch the limit, split the loaf, hang with the homeboys, solve the puzzle, feed the rat. Maybe. But purpose is not the point. It is the doing—not the having done—and, of course, the *un*doing that matters most.

The road ends where I arrive. Trembling on caffeine and carbohydrates I turn off the headlights and sit for a long time listening to the dust settle. The sun will be up before long. I finish my coffee and a bagel, then walk to the back of the truck and take out my pack. A coyote yips at the moon-shadowed length of me. Other than that there is nothing.

were all we saw in those days, and the style of the times dictated that we scrape our way through the lichen with wire brushes and screwdrivers never allowing the rope to bear our weight, or resting on our protection. Those were the rules and we took them seriously. Though as the years went by and our hunger grew we began to realize that these regulations were not the word of God. They were tools, a path that one could choose to take or ignore. So we started rapping new routes to clean them out, tossing away loose stones and chucking off garbage. Occasionally we would rehearse a move on rappel, but for the most part we were honest about our transgressions, and the more honest we were, the less anyone seemed to care.

But like most purity, ours was poorly designed for compromise. As more people came and the competition for new routes grew, the greatest victories seemed to fall to those with the fewest scruples. Soon we were all hang-dogging and pre-placing gear. What we surrendered in mystery was returned to us in the form of new expertise. Our standards accelerated so fast that by the mid-1980s all the cracks had been climbed out. We had nowhere left to look but to the spaces between our routes. You hear about the Europeans and "French free" and all that crap, but that's not the way it was. We were pioneers. What we discovered out there we discovered on our own. And it astonished us. The edges and knobs had always been there, of course, but we had had neither the eyes to see nor the technology to take us there.

Now, as we threw ourselves at harder and harder problems we realized that the ancient art of hand-driving bolts while hanging from skyhooks no longer applied. It was then that the first power drills arrived. Equipped with modern mechanics but still chained to the "ground up" ethics of the past we first tried using a Bosche on the lead. In most cases this meant climbing with a haul line, finding a stance from which the drill could be hauled, and then leveling it with one hand against the rock. Once the hole was complete the drill was lowered and a $^5/_8$-inch bolt driven, torqued, and caulked. Then, the rope was threaded and, if the leader had any strength left, the drill brought back up and hung from the bolt with a Fifi hook. Thankfully, it did not take long for this process to collapse of its own weight. By 1986 we were down-bolting our way over roofs and hand-crafting new possibilities as we went. Then everybody bought drills and the pace of development exploded.

By the early 1990s the place was played out as far as most of us were concerned. The parking lot was paved, port-a-potties had appeared, and on any given weekend SUVs lined both sides of the road for nearly a mile. It was our fault and we knew it. Disgusted with what our ambitions had wrought, we abandoned the country we had opened and went looking for our own nether-Eden. It took two years before we discovered the Amphitheater. This time we agreed to do it differently. This time, we agreed to do it right.

Over the months that followed we installed environmentally conscious trails, edging our paths with rock work and benches, boxing in steps where the approach was too steep to hold a tread, and hauling away enough debris to hide our cars. And, of course, we climbed. Only this time we started with the faces. Placing our bolts so as neither to discriminate against the short of stature nor to overly placate the feckless, we created over two dozen routes of stunning difficulty and aesthetic worth. We raided our savings and placed chains at the top of each route in order to spare ourselves the indignation of a long walk back to the base. We installed a box latrine in the shade of a juniper tree and flattened out a spot for camping. We allowed no fires for fear of discovery and chastened anyone who confessed the urge to bring in friends. Still, by early in the autumn we realized the end was in sight. We agreed to one last project each, two last days.

am at play among the overhangs until the others arrive. I rap back down to the ground and we eat breakfast together. The mood is convivial, bright. And once the sun has warmed the rock we split up into pairs to set about our separate swan songs. I belay until noon, at which point my companion throws a final dead point and hooks the rim. He is still laughing when I lower him to the ground. We hang around the campsite during the heat of the day and tell stories. I dose until 3 P.M., then gather my quick draws and a new belayer. We walk back up to the crag without talking.

The prow of rock that I have come to climb begins in the back of a cave where a wide crack cleaves an overhanging staircase into separate hemispheres. The first crux is off the ground, but I have bouldered it so many times my mind moves almost automatically to the climbing above. That is a mistake. I fall twice before reaching the roof. I ask to be lowered to the ground, untie, and pull my rope through. I stretch and sit in the sunlight re-taping my fingers and trying to clear my mind. I concentrate on the smell of the grass, the breeze that curls over the edge of the cliff. The view of the river. When my breathing has calmed I start thinking about the route again. I take a deep breath, look back up, and smile. I don't know why but there is something funny about having had such high expectations and having fallen off so low. Irony that even I can't avoid laughing at. My belayer pats me on the back when I return to the rope. "What the hell?" she says, and I look at her and nod and say, "What the hell?"

This time it all goes as if by plan. Crimps and cruxes come and go, my feet find their marks, and although the climbing is hard—perhaps the hardest climbing I have ever done—hitting the chains feels more like fulfillment than triumph. There isn't a victory scream inside me anywhere. I hesitate at the top, turning to take one last look at the route from above, then ask to be lowered.

It is 6 P.M. by the time we have all gathered back at the campsite. We put up our tents, lay out our sleeping bags and eat dinner. We talk like climbers. Four new routes to make a total of twenty-nine, though our conjecture is suspect. Nobody has written anything down. We haven't given anything names or numbers. Our goal from the beginning has been to leave it the way we found it. To play and then go away.

As darkness falls we divide our tasks for the next day. There is much discussion on the varied techniques of erasure. We laugh and tell lies and drink a bottle of champagne. By 11 P.M. we have settled into our sleeping bags. The raven's breast sky is spread with the dust of a billion galaxies. We lie on our backs and look up at the night and think ourselves to be the luckiest people on the planet.

ALL FREE ON THE VMC

...Despite present day fears of the tendency to replace substance with glitter, virtuosity is still at hand.

standards and eyebrows everywhere they went, the trio also managed to produce several enduring classics—not the least of which is the Vulgarian Mountain Club Direct (V 5.9, A3), a surprisingly *indirect* line up the center of Cannon Mountain's 1,000-foot east face.

Such was the reputation of the first-ascent party that it took nearly four years for someone to straighten out their work. Nailing a disconnected series of right-facing corners, Steve Arsenault (on leave from duty in Vietnam) and Sam Streibert climbed directly to the VMC's fourth belay over two rainy days in the spring of 1969. Their new line—straighter and cleaner than the original—immediately became known as the Direct-Direct and for many years thereafter was considered the big wall route to do on Cannon. A reputation it still held when Scottish ice master Malcolm Fraser and I arrived late in the summer of 1973. Fresh off an epic nine-hour approach in my dilapidated VW bus, we turned our gaze on the cliff just in time to witness the local SAR group removing the bodies of two young climbers from a route named Sam's Swan Song. With that sobering image in mind, and with little experience as aid climbers, our progress on the route the following day was, to be charitable, sluggish. A night spent standing in etriers as a cold rain poured down the inside of our plastic rain jackets did nothing for our morale. Late in the afternoon of our second day we dragged the tattered remains of our haul sack across the summit slabs, both of us vowing never to return.

I lied. Twenty years later I was back. Climbing free and carrying only "a rope, a rack, and the shirts on our backs," Malcolm MacCormick and I ticked the route all free in just under four hours.

—

While occasional parties still undertake the "Double D" as a big wall aid project,[2] it has reached its maturity as an outstanding free climb (IV 5.10+). Done either way, the route rarely disappoints anyone. Its gear-gobbling cracks, directness of line, and satisfying geometry have earned it a reputation as a route of extraordinary quality. A career achievement for climbers of moderate ability even dedicated sportsters will suffer the long approach simply to take down the first five pitches. Although a full rack of climbing gear is required, fixed gear appears when needed, and all the belays are comfortable. Owing to Cannon's slightly less than vertical nature, photographic opportunities abound. At nine pitches and slightly more than 1,000 feet in length, it must be considered not only one of the longest routes in the east, but surely one of the best.

In 1975, when Malcolm (Fraser, not MacCormick) and I limped down the descent path in our mud-soaked PAs it was the route we blamed for our incompetence. Twenty years later, walking off felt very different. Less like revenge than growing up. A time to reflect on all the climbs, the friends, and miles that had come between. And the only adjective that came to mind was "splendid."

---

[2] *Climbed on aid, the route goes clean at IV* 5.8, *C*2.

BUILT ON ROCK

If I walk away from this, he thought, I'll be an old man—all ghosts and hangovers and mellow recollections. Fuck it, he thought, follow the blood. This

intuition, every heartbeat. It was, he would say later, the second best idea he'd ever had. The best, of course, was to go climbing in the first place.

As to the question of how a tow-headed Irish kid elbowing out his adolescence on the hard pavement of South Boston ever wound up walking home with a Heinrich Harrer book tucked under his arm in the first place is still something of a mystery. Fate? A progressive librarian? Nobody knows for sure, but that was most definitely the beginning of it. Mead Cunningham, age fifteen, lying on his bed with *The White Spider* spread open across his chest while visions of clear-eyed Teutonic youths carrying rucksacks and alpenstocks danced in his head. Images that a week later would have him hitchhiking north intent upon climbing Mount Washington in the dead of winter. A poor plan, he would later admit, considering that his entire expedition kit consisted of two cans of Hormel chili, a canteen, a jackknife, and two extra pairs of cotton socks for his PF Flyers. Jammed in a nylon gym bag were, in addition to the blue jeans and wool pea jacket he was wearing, some cotton work gloves and a woolen watch cap. Suicidal, perhaps, but considering that the whole idea of the climb was based more on what he was trying to get away from than what he was trying to get to, the lack of proper equipment was only a minor deterrent. Mead's life at home was the kind that inspired hasty departures. What with one parent throwing bottles and the other talking to them, the prospects of freezing to death in Huntington Ravine seemed almost appealing in comparison. Not that Mead was entirely without pity for his parents. He'd simply had enough, that's all. Watching the old man sink into booze while his mother drifted into madness was just no longer very entertaining.

Fortunately, he was saved in his folly by a pair of AMC instructors who later made room for him in their basic climbing class and, over Easter weekend, took him up the Standard Route on White Horse Rock. From there on, Mead Cunningham needed no further encouragement. He was hooked. His thin body and barely controlled rage found a pertinence on rock he'd never experienced on the scuffling streets of Bean Town. A glimmering madness. So he invested the totality of his life's savings in a pair of used climbing shoes, a cheap harness, and a locking carabiner. He hand-stitched a chalk bag out of material he found in his mother's sewing drawer, constructed a practice wall on the back of their building, and put a pull-up bar in the basement. No weekend was too cold or rainy to keep him at home, no partner too unskilled or overly ambitious to intimidate him. He was consumed by rock. Absorbed in a world that paralleled that of his parents and classmates but touched them only in passing. A finer, truer, and more meaningful place as far as he was concerned. A place in comparison to which his last two years of high school seemed more like an extension of childhood than a step in the direction of maturity. It was an utter mystery to his parents. A waste, according to his teachers who bemoaned such a misapplication of intelligence. For his part, Mead accepted their entreaties like a man trying his best to understand a language with which he shared no vocabulary, and he sustained himself on a diet of mountaineering books and magazines into the margins of which he inscribed poetry of ascent and the detailed topographical sketches of every route he had ever done.

The day after graduation he told his parents he was moving out. The old man went on a brilliant bender over that one, raving through half the night about having sired a gorilla and trashing the house. His mother made him brownies. The next morning he put the brownies in a bag, threw his K-Mart backpack over his shoulder, and hitched a ride to North Conway. He found a job there washing dishes and slept in the woods until he'd saved enough money to rent a room within bicycling distance of the crags. He made friends with some other climbers and

Only the thrill had changed. As his skill...

rock less in its geologic context and more as a series of personal riddles. Something inside him awaiting release. He made several trips to England during this period and one to the Dolomites. He went home only once. It was not a pleasant visit. There was nothing left there for him. No clothes in the closet, no place at the table, no joy in Mudville. His final farewell amounted to a kiss on the cheek for Mum and a fuck you for Father. After that there was no going back; just a future that stretched out as far and wide as the whole Himalaya.

When his girlfriend got into graduate school at the University of Colorado Mead decided to move out to Boulder with her. When they broke up he came back east for a year, then wound up returning to Boulder on his own terms. The drive from New Hampshire to Colorado was instructive. It gave Mead a chance to cast a long view out over his life and consider what lay ahead. He was not unhappy with what he saw. He was twenty-eight, climbing solid 5.12, and fit as a horse. He couldn't imagine doing anything that would make him happier. Yet neither could he imagine doing what he was doing indefinitely. By the time he reached Boulder he understood that it was only a stopover, not a destination. He got a room on Pearl Street and a job at one of the local climbing shops but he did not remove his possessions from the two rucksacks in which they fit. Mead knew there had to be more.

The idea of going to Yosemite occurred to him almost as an

afterthought. It was a notion that, once considered, percolated inside him; it was as if the decision had already been made long ago. Of course talking about the Valley was considered to be incredibly *un*cool in Boulder in those days, so Mead kept his musing to himself. But if climbing was the faith that held Mead's life together, Yosemite was his St. Peters. The pilgrimage was mandatory. Night after night he sat in his room thumbing through the pages of the guidebook, studying it like a liturgy, and committing its routes to memory in the fashion of an idiot savant with a gift for corners, cracks, dihedrals, and ceilings. By the time he actually got in his car and headed west it seemed as if he was going somewhere familiar. That complacency ended the minute he drove through the gate at El Portal. The air seemed to whoosh out of him like he'd been jolted by electricity. The dust and light, the smile on the face of the ranger who waved him through the gate, the scent of fir and melting snow, the gut-shrinking vastness of El Capitan—it was all as if he had been waiting all his life to be there.

His original plan had been to stay a month. He wound up staying the entire summer. In all that time his daily regime never changed. Between sun up and sun down he climbed. Night meant getting high, sorting gear, working out or walking back to Camp 4 on feet too swollen to fit in his shoes after some over-ambitious epic. That was it. No clock, no calendar, no cares. He invested whole weeks in secret projects that he completed and walked away from without naming. Always conservative about risk he now found himself running it out on the subglacial shoeshine of Middle Cathedral, hanging out in the horizonless space of El Cap, fingertips and toe jams holding him to the rock, his balls shrinking in his guts, and the whole universe reduced to the scale of dime-sized edges and pimpled rugosites. Crazy to live and crazy to climb, Mead both lost and found himself on that vertical seascape and he might have stayed in Yosemite forever had he not run out of money.

As it was, he returned to Boulder with less than $15 in his pocket and a mountain of debts in the mailbox. He did double duty that winter, washing dishes at night and selling climbing gear by day until by March he had saved enough to think about another trip to the Valley. He had also decided to take his college board exams. If climbing was his muse, his hands were his tools, and they were just about fed up with washing dishes. He knew he couldn't afford C.U. so he applied to the University

Mead felt sure they would enjoy each other—which they did, arriving in the Valley a week late and shuffling their feet with embarrassment. But so enraptured was Mead that he did not recognize the pie-in-the-face infidelity of his two closest friends until he was told. Then he did the only thing he knew how to do. He packed up his belongings and left.

He did not stop until he reached the coast of Maine. It was still early in the tourist season when he arrived so it was easy for him to get work. He found a job in the kitchen of a Bar Harbor seafood restaurant and rented a room over the local climbing shop. When he was ready to look, he discovered that Acadia National Park was fat with rock. He spent the whole summer climbing and it is possible that he might, too, have stayed in Bar Harbor had it not been for the application he had submitted to the university. When he received word that he had been accepted Mead decided to give college a try. He was twenty-nine years old and it was time, he reasoned, to learn something. He piled as many credits as he could into twice-weekly commutes from Bar Harbor to Bangor and had been at that schedule for almost four years when the second-best notion of his life occurred to him.

It did not, as it did for Zarathrustra, knock him on his cosmogonical ass. It came to him in the form of a blown fan belt. He was driving across the Brewster Bridge when he heard the thing rip and saw his generator light flash on. Gravity was on his side, however, and he was able to coast downhill to a service station where he was told they could have it fixed in an hour. It took more like two. He'd read all their back copies of *Life* and *People* in less than fifteen minutes so there wasn't much to do other than walk outside. Twenty strides to the south he found himself standing in front of the defunct sepulchre of the First Avenue Presbyterian Church.

The next afternoon he came back and walked through the building with a real estate agent. The structure was not in good repair. Most of its windows were broken and the pews were warped with mildew. Cobwebs hung like angel hair from its beams and its 40-foot stone walls were black with industrial grit. A faded sign reading, "Do Not Enter on Pain of Prosecution" hung by a single nail from the front door.

Mead left for Boston that afternoon. He got a haircut, shaved off his moustache, put on a borrowed suit, and arrived at his Uncle Sydney's office an hour ahead of his appointment. Sydney Schiffer was his mother's older brother, the favor-giver of the Schiffer clan, and the heartwood of the family tree. Rotund, brooding, and difficult, Uncle Sydney had inherited a large fortune through his wife and quadrupled it by means of shrewd investments and hardball expense control. He met Mead in the library. He was wearing a brown suit, smoking a cigar, and clearly did not recognize his only begotten nephew. As Mead spoke, Uncle Sydney stared at him from behind thick wire-framed glasses and issued large clouds of gray exhaust from his hairy nostrils. When he spoke he rolled his Rs like olives. He would, he declared, out of affection for his lunatic sister, make Mead the loan of $8,000. In addition, he would allow Mead to borrow another $12,000 over the next twelve months at 9 percent interest. Mead thanked him and walked outside uncertain of everything other than the fact that forty-eight hours after the first time he had ever walked inside one, Mead Cunningham was the owner of a church.

He spent the winter working like a saint alone inside that cold shell of faith. He gutted the building, tearing out everything but the original maple flooring. He took down the south-facing half of the roof and let the snow come in while he worked to replace the ceiling with a huge puzzle of Plexiglas sky lights. He built an 8-foot-wide box along the interior base of the wall and, in the spring, ran guerilla raids to every beach within 100 miles to fill it with 6 inches of fine, soft sand. He hand drilled more than a hundred 4-inch Rawl drive bolts, placing them at 2-foot intervals along the top of the wall and painting numbers, 1 through

front foyer. He also had forty-one routes established and graded. With another grand from Uncle Sydney he bought seventy pair of Korean EBs and three dozen harnesses. He printed a guide to the walls, color-coded the routes, and bought 200 T-shirts emblazoned with his logo and the phrase, "I did it all at Cunningham Crags!" One week before his grand opening he went to visit a Portland-based human potential organization called "Life/Hope" and talked them into renting the building two evenings a month for their basic training course. A psychiatrist at Eastern Maine Medical Center rented it another eight days a month for his youth counseling program. Down to his final $1,500, Mead ran ads in every newspaper in Maine and on every college-oriented FM radio station in the state.

When the doors finally opened a small crowd of mostly high-school-age customers entered and walked around with their mouths hanging open. The next night the Portland and Bangor papers showed up along with several television crews. By the weekend it seemed as if half of Bangor was trying to get in. It was a shame Mead was not there to see it. He was down in Boston visiting Uncle Sydney and talking to him about buying a church in Cambridge.

PART II
Journeys

INTO FALL

Every pain has a story.

—Atul Gawande

Θ

June was the last good month. The monsoons had come and gone and the forest was lush with ferns and orchids and billowing lakes of elephant grass. The sky was blue and cloudless. The days were long and warm. At night we sat outside our bunkers drinking stale coffee and staring west across a broad plain to duplicate mountains on the far horizon.

In the mornings haze covered the plateau, setting the peaks afloat like purple islands on a sea of white spume. Skeins of parakeets flew in the fog, and monkeys leapt back and forth among the naked branches of dead trees. We built showers and a chapel. A sergeant from the first platoon traded us stew made out of C-rations boiled in a discarded steel helmet for cigarettes. Laundry slapped on guy-lines. Helicopters brought in our mail and hot food and, once, two middle-aged men and three young women in crisp powder-blue uniforms who told us they were from the Red Cross. They were cheerful and overweight and in love with the war. Their desire to make it all great fun felt like bad luck, and many of those who had been on the hill the longest stayed away. They served us supper from insulated Marmite canisters, and then the women sat drinking coffee with the officers while the two men passed among the leftover eaters asking them about their hometowns and girlfriends. When the helicopters returned they apologized about having to go and stood on the landing pad waving as if to old friends. No one waved back and no one hooted when the prop-blast threw up the skirts of the three young women to thick mid-Iowa thighs. The circle of soldiers who had come down to bid them goodbye simply stared in silence, following the lights of the departing ship until it disappeared into darkness.

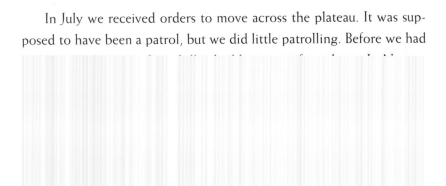

In July we received orders to move across the plateau. It was supposed to have been a patrol, but we did little patrolling. Before we had

cans, shovels, mortar rounds, extra hand grenades, and wooden crates of
rifle ammunition. We slung our weapons over our shoulders and walked
heads down, counting steps. We moved carelessly through abandoned
enemy camps and kicked through their dead fires without alarm. The
heat grew. Men passed out and were revived and passed out again. There
was no sound other than the squelch of the radios and the drumming of
distant artillery.

After five days we reached the other side of the plateau, climbed the
first mountain we came to, and set our camp on its summit. We cut down
the trees, burned off the grass, dug holes in which to live and filled sandbags with which to cover the holes. The helicopters came with huge
rolls of barbed wire, cardboard cases of C-rations and pale-skinned replacements in stiff new fatigues. By the end of the month we could look
out through the turrets of our new bunkers and see across the valley to
the mountain where we had been a month before. We were adrift behind
moving walls but safe again and strangely distant from the shooting.

On the last day of July the battalion commander's helicopter exploded as it approached the perimeter. No one heard incoming fire or
saw a rocket. It just blew up: smoking pieces of metal spinning off in a
dozen crazy arches as the fiery bulk of the machine dropped into the
trees. The captain sent out a couple of patrols to search for the wreckage, but they didn't find anything. Some LURPS tried to find it, too, and

came back empty-handed. It was as if the jungle had swallowed it whole. Bad *ju-ju*, the Bloods told us. The shit is coming down.

We got more replacements in August. In every group there were a few cooks or typists or mechanics from the rear who had forgotten to salute or polish their boots or make their beds and had been punished by being sent forward to die. Along with the replacements came new orders. We were directed to increase the number of patrols we had in the field. The patrols were to stay out longer in their search for the enemy. They were to avoid, if at all possible, any direct contact. The idea, as our Captain explained it, was to find Charlie, then bring in enough troops to make him stand and fight.

In the beginning some patrols actually managed to spot concentrations of enemy soldiers, sneak back into the bushes, and radio in their reports. More often, though, they simply wandered around aimlessly in the jungle, never seeing or hearing anything, cut off, helpless, and frightened witless. Some with less luck blundered into ambushes or silently vanished. We lost ten men in twenty days, twenty in less than a month. Rumors began circulating about patrols crawling out a few hundred meters into the jungle and hiding until it was time to come back in. Conversations died. Hash ate the evenings.

In September there was no rain. The wind turned to dust. We wore masks of red clay and waited. The enemy had begun an offensive aimed at clearing his supply routes to the south and the eye of the war moved toward us. The shelling began on the first day of October. For three days and nights they bombarded our hilltop with mortars and rockets and artillery while we fired our mortars back at them and our planes dropped bombs and napalm. The jungle burned and the sky filled with black smoke. No one dared to go outside, not even to piss. We crouched in the corners of our bunkers without eating or sleeping, huddled inside helmets and flak jackets while the rats went crazy and ran in mad circles, spilling blood out of their ears and flecking the sandbags with red.

On the fourth night of the barrage their big guns worked our mortar pits and then rolled downhill to focus on the bunkers guarding the low side of the line. No one was surprised when their infantry came up the hill, crawling at first, then screaming and hurling themselves against our

struggles of fingernails and knives.

Then, as abruptly as it had begun, it was over. The thing was gone. The shooting stopped and morning came up orange and Michigan blue. Our captain came out and stood at the top of the hill and screamed with his face turned up to the sky and only then did we abandon our broken works, rising one by one from the destruction of our city on the hill to gape at its waste. There was no shape left to the world that I could remember, no familiar contour, no form to its past or future. Around us the disassembled bodies of the dead and dying lay tangled in the wire. The vandalized jungle smoked in its ruin, carrying on its upland breeze the fragrances of dark garages and dead leaves, the scents of summer and youth, the dank aroma of cordite, blood, sawdust, and death.

The jets and helicopters came back in packs. Our own dead and wounded were carried down to the landing pad in a crusade of poncho litters and black-bagged remains. Some of the survivors smoked borrowed cigarettes and laughed. Others sat with their heads down or held hands with boys whose faces were puzzled with pain and gray from morphine. The unwrapped enemy were last in line. The division commander arrived by helicopter and walked among them with a grim expression on his face. When he reached our wounded he smiled and began stooping every few feet to shake hands with busted boys who tried to straighten out on their litters into a position of attention. A young sergeant in tailored fatigues snapped pictures of the general as he posed above the ruins of a blackened bunker, holding an enemy rifle and nudging the body of a dead enemy officer with the toe of his boot. When more shooting broke out a few hundred meters below our position the general decided to leave but only with great reluctance. As his helicopter lifted off, he saluted and the sergeant took a few last photographs. Then he put down his cameras and turned to await a ride out on one of the ships bringing in our mail and hot food.

After we had eaten and read our letters from home the captain announced that we would be moving out again. His voice was quiet and he did not meet us with his eyes. We were to be a blocking force, he said, his voice sinking to a whisper. But no one complained. Nothing was said. We just sat there in our small groups and passed around cigarettes or tins of C-ration fruit. Some of the guys dropped down on their backs and tried to sleep, reaching into their dreams after things they could no longer fully remember. Then it began to rain. Lightly, at first, finally in a steady downpour. Shortly before noon the old man gave the sign and we all stood up, stubbed out our cigarettes, and started down the hill, stumbling and glissading in the mud, slipping once more into the jungle's embrace.

MAKALU, TOO.
WOULDN'T YOU?

Do you need to be told that even such modest attainments as you can

The West Face of Makalu (27,850 feet) intimidates on sight. Preeminent among the climbing world's last great problems, it is 10,000 feet of frozen granite, bullet-hard ice, and falling debris. An alpine wall that, since its discovery, has remained among the least traveled of vertical spaces.

Our original plan had been to climb something else. Not another peak—from the beginning we knew we wanted to climb Makalu—just another route. Early on we had thought about repeating either its Northwest Ridge or the less technical Southeast Ridge. Each had the appeal of offering a direct shot at the summit and the strong likelihood of being able to put somebody on top. The more we talked about it, however, the clearer it became that few of us were really interested in going halfway around the world to follow in someone else's footsteps. Our attention then shifted to the unclimbed South Face, but that hope, too, was dashed when a Yugoslavian expedition succeeded on the route just prior to our arrival. So with tickets in hand, gear shipped, and permits in place, we changed plans. Based on a single photograph and the wildest of post-adolescent optimism we decided to head west and into the unknown.

We had hardly hired our porters before we found the full forces of the mountain turned against us. It was that kind of expedition. The trails were muddy, the locals ill-humored, and the critical bridges in poor repair. Rain fell upon us without mercy. Rain that translated to heavy snows up high that meant frostbitten feet for our porters and two days of trench-ing our way across slopes creaking with avalanche danger simply to establish our base camp. Then there was the wind. By setting up house in the shadow of the mountain's darkest architecture we found we had subjected ourselves to a micro-climate of hurricane downdrafts and pierc-ing cold. Conditions that rattled the frames of our most stout tents and settled a chill over us for which even our state-of-the-art sleeping bags were no match. Our location hurt us in other ways, too. With the thin thread of our logistical resources already stretched taut by the exagger-ated scale of the landscape, we found ourselves compelled to place base camp at 18,500 feet—too distant, as it turned out, to either resupply from the valley or allow adequate recovery from the rigors of the face.

In view of all this it is tempting to say that we never had a chance. Yet, in truth, our demise probably lay as much in mind as it did in matter. The difference between good intentions and a Himalayan summit is measured in will. Food, tools, and favorable weather carry you only so far. After that, the outcome is decided by desire. And although the idea of standing atop the world's fifth highest peak certainly had its appeal, if we were plump with want, we were perhaps somewhat slender in our passion.

Like members of all expeditions, the people on our team had been drawn together by a wide variety of ambitions. For some, the trip was the fulfillment of a long climbing career. For others, it was the next logi-cal step. In a society of geographical morons, both groups knew that the segue from life as a big name among the lesser ranges to international credibility meant capping an 8,000-meter peak. Makalu was to be that stepping stone. But our largest contingent had no such ambitions. For them the trip was nothing more than an adventure. They had nothing to prove, no burden of reputation to defend. Only the pure and simple desire to ride the high as far as it went. They talked openly about the expedition as a kind of low-rent semester abroad, only funkier and with better drugs. They would carry loads and string ropes as long as the climbing was cool, but they had few hopes for the summit and no intentions whatsoever of giving up their lives in the process. Along with these bicameral camps came the usual collection of tag-alongs and money-lenders. The temporary culture of mixed emotions, deep pockets, and love relationships that always accompanies an expedition in the field.

base camp sank into malaise, so too did we press the route, slowly moving rope, food, gear, and fuel up the face. Camps were installed, problems solved, and the mind-numbing work of hauling loads accomplished. Enough that by the end of our first month on the mountain we had put the worst of the barriers below us and reached a point of decision.

All of which is to say that we were probably your normal, everyday, run-of-the-mill Himalayan expedition. A loose confederation of freelance adventurers who awaken one day to find themselves caught between daring and desire, half afraid of going on and half afraid of going back, overawed, underwhelmed, and grievously confused; an alpine Woodstock ten-day's walk from the nearest relief with nothing to do but roll the dice and nowhere to go but up.

⌐⌐

It was a point I reached by accident. I had been sitting at home one night when the phone rang and I heard the voice of an old acquaintance on the other end of the line. We had climbed a wall in Yosemite together some years earlier but had been in only sporadic communication since. He had confused my phone number for someone else's. But, after exchanging pleasantries and correcting the mistake, he allowed as how he had recently acquired a permit for Makalu and was putting together a team. Would I care to go? Could I raise some money? Would I mind assembling some gear? Like Molly Bloom on creatine I was whispering "Yes, yes, God yes" before he'd even finished. After that we discussed dates, possible routes, and an inventory of equipment, then said goodbye and that was pretty much it. No blood tests, no references, no résumé. In fact, I hardly heard another peep out of him for the next five months. Just a few phone calls, a couple postcards, and an airplane ticket. It wasn't until I arrived in Kathmandu three days late and $90 the poorer for having tried to bribe an Indian customs official that I started feeling like I was really going on an expedition. A point of view quickly corroborated by the fact that I was standing in the ninety-degree heat wearing double boots, a down parka, and toting an eighty-pound carry-on full of climbing gear.

Inauspicious beginnings are a specialty of mine, and I would not have imagined a big trip starting in any more appropriate fashion. If my previous visits to the Far East had taught me anything it was to stay open to omens. To pay attention to the little things. Indeed, the seventy-two hours of penance I had already spent in the departure lounge of the Delhi airport had amply demonstrated to me that in India even something as seemingly innocent as a smile can house many textures of meaning. Thus, having caught a cab into the city, I advanced upon the Kathmandu Guest House and the first meeting with my fellow expeditioners with catlike trepidation.

"Oh, Mr. Childs," shouted the clerk behind the reception desk the moment I entered, "We are so glad to be seeing you!" A jowl-stretching grin traversed his face and I stretched my mind to recall if we had ever met before. "Your friends, you know, they are already here!" he nodded enthusiastically, gesturing toward a door and spinning the registration book toward me. "Yes, yes, they are all out on the veranda," he continued. "Oh, they are going to be so happy to be seeing you!" He was still nodding as I picked up my bags and headed out through the door.

Now I confess that the reading I had done in preparation for this trip had, to some extent, seeded a number of unrealistic expectations in my mind. Dragging my gear down a long hallway I imagined turning a corner and finding a courtyard filled with the sepia-toned forms of gaunt faced Anglo-Saxons wearing pith helmets and jodhpurs, sipping tea and leaning over dog-eared maps marked "Terra Incognita." What I discovered, instead, was a dozen long-haired young men standing in an advanced state of undress among the str...

rest were Yankee hardwood, our alpine elite, the superheroes of my sport.

We introduced ourselves, divided tasks, and as the day wore on I began to feel more at ease. For dinner, all eighteen of us gathered to hear our leader detail the strategy of our climb. The plan, as he explained it, would be to divide our assault into three tiers. The first would consist of the two Yugoslavs, both Himalayan veterans, and the two most experienced Americans. A second tier of six climbers would haul in support of the first team, and a third tier would haul in support of them. As weather, fitness, acclimatization, and luck staggered our ranks, he continued, we would mix the teams with the goal of keeping the strongest players closest to the front.

It all seemed very logical to me. But as the beer flowed and we stood around gabbing in the codified language of inquiry that climbers use to evaluate one another, it became increasingly clear to me that there was no one even amongst the third tier of climbers with a résumé weaker than my own. Other details also floated to the surface. There were not, for instance, enough wind suits and sleeping bags to go around. Same with packs. Furthermore, a second entourage of climbers were now slated to arrive three weeks into the trip. The hope was that their late arrival would turbo-charge our final push for the summit. In my desultory state of mind, however, they only threatened to push me further in the direction of latrine duty. By the time we adjourned for the night I was feeling about as welcome as a welfare mother at a Jessie Helms fundraiser. Though I was more absolutely certain than ever that we would climb the mountain, I was utterly resigned to the fact that my chances of getting anywhere on it were nil.

I shouldn't have worried.

We had hardly come together before we began falling apart. As the days and nights of our approach proceeded it became apparent that we were a whole composed of many parts that did not necessarily fit together well. Along with our 175 porters there were among us ethno-cultists and cultural imperialists, tea drinkers and drug abusers, the funny and the foolish, those with whom any connection at all was impossible and those with whom it was impossible not to connect. We were a Noah's Ark of civilized quirks; a walking exploration of why, with all the reasons big expeditions fail represented in the pool of our talent and eccentricities.

On the other hand, the approach march itself was spectacular. With light packs and all day to kill, I would get up early, hike for two or three hours, and then stop at a tea house to read and eat or take photographs. Children and amber light accompanied me everywhere. The worst of the rains fell while I waited under thatched roofs. Monsoon clouds still gripped the high peaks but that only made it easier to focus on the scenery close at hand. Everywhere I looked there was something spectacular: shafts of smoking sunlight, the deep green of the jungle, the hand-tilled fields and mists swirling in the river bottoms. I felt immersed in magic. Even the languid gymnastics of the leeches held poetry.

But already things were beginning to go wrong. Gear was stolen and our medical supplies vandalized. A cow destroyed one of our tents. Porters quit or suffered injury. And then somewhere in between the last Hindu village and the first Sherpa settlement our physician went mad. His eccentricities had always been pronounced, but suddenly they seemed to take a turn into a darkness from which he never fully returned. When the two American members of our first team quit the expedition within one hour of each other it almost seemed anti-climactic. Our leader called a meeting complete with tears and accusations about personal space and intestinal problems, but in the end they had already made up their minds to leave and that was that. I got my sleeping bag and wind suit. Our liaison officer, who had been spending too much time with the doctor,

we were depending on them." I did not disagree. My name was now among the members of the second tier and I was feeling an unusual generosity of spirit. In fact, with the mountain in view and the worst of our approach behind us, we were all beginning to feel a lot better. The doctor was self-medicating, the weather was fair, and the team of Japanese climbers laying siege to Baruntse had welcomed us to the headwaters of the Arun with enough food and alcohol to dispel whatever acrimony existed between those who had decided to stay on. The last night before our push to base camp we stood outside under a full moon and gazed up at Makalu and joked that perhaps we would have the thing done before our reinforcements had even arrived. It was a horribly naïve statement. But brought up in a world where our every hunger had always been fed we had no reason to believe that our dream would go unanswered. Hate us for our arrogance if you will, but forgive us our innocence.

⸺

In legend, Makalu is a minor God with a reputation for being tough on good intentions. Over the years his granite counterpart has done its best to live up to that notoriety. Its easiest routes have turned back the strongest of climbers. Those who have aspired to ascend its more difficult features have been treated even worse. Perhaps because we aspired to climb its fiercest geography, and because it thought us weak, the West

Face showed us no forgiveness at all. Our every indiscretion, every lapse of judgment was punished with inordinate severity. Crevasses opened beneath our feet. The snow fell relentlessly. Fevers, bronchitis, blood clots, and HAPE attacked us in our sleep. During the days our feet froze and an intestinal bug so ravaged our bowels that Lomotil outpaced Darvon as the after-dinner drug of choice. The higher we went, the worse it became. Camp II—our jumping-off point for moving food and equipment to the more technical terrain above—burned to the ground in a stove explosion. We ran out of toilet paper. Storms nailed us in place when we most needed to be moving, and attrition so savaged our ranks that even I was soon looking forward to the arrival of our second entourage. By the end of our sixth week on the hill only the two Yugoslavs were left climbing out front with me hauling in support. Camp III, a two-person tent into which the three of us now crammed ourselves, was re-christened the Death Box after all three of us were hit by rockfall during a single twenty-four-hour period while laying inside. We moved it twice but sleeping in that tent remained an experience akin to lying down beneath the executioner's blade. We knew the second ice field would offer better shelter, but after four days of climbing we arrived at the end of our rope supply 200 feet short of our objective. With tools too bent and dull for climbing we had no choice but to descend for replacements.

It was a much-dreaded decision. With momentum finally seeming to shift in our direction we did not want to go back. Reaching the second ice field marked our longest sustained advance. Yet we could not proceed without rope or better equipment. After a long discussion with our leader over the radio we decided we had no alternative but to descend.

The world to which we returned was much changed from the one we had left. Snow had melted out from around our base camp tent and lines of colorful prayer flags snapped in the wind. Smoke curled from the cook tent and we could hear the voices of our Sherpa kitchen staff shouting over the roar of their stoves. We had hardly sat down before they brought us cookies and cups of steaming tea. No one from the base camp tent even stuck his head out to offer a greeting.

Inside we found in place of our once proud and happy team the wounded and demoralized remains of an army in defeat. Whatever sense of community had once existed between those who climbed and those who waited was now gone. With nothing left t~ ~~~~ ~~~~~~~ ~ ~

struck them as nothing other than a selfish attempt to drag out the inevitable at the potential cost of someone's life. There was no screaming but there was no agreement, either. Eventually, a few of our colleagues volunteered for another carry to Camp I but only if it would help move things along. They had no enthusiasm for it. No hunger. It was the same dichotomy of desire that I have since learned every big expedition encounters at the moment when the decision to go on or to go back hangs in judgment.

In our case, the prospect of the arrival of a second band of healthy climbers tilted the balance in favor of one last try. The second entourage, our leader pointed out, was now acclimatizing at our South Face camp. In two days they would be in base, and in another forty-eight hours carrying supplies to Camp I. That meant we could have our shot. It was all the hope we needed. We began packing immediately. The plan was for the two Yugoslavs to start first. They would haul double loads to Camp III where I would meet them a day later. Then one of us would descend to Camp I to meet the new arrivals while the other two made a haul to the top of our fixed lines. Once Camp IV was in place we would make an alpine-style run for the summit.

My night in base camp after the Yugoslavs had gone up was less awkward. The decision had been made; there was an end in sight and people were happy. We smoked pot and played cards. I wrote some letters home and did some repair work on my gear. Then, after everyone else had gone to bed, I sat in the big tent and talked with our leader. He expressed his concern for us and then spoke at length about his family and children. It was the first time I understood how hard it was for him to find himself suspended between competing circumstance for which he felt responsibility but over which he had no power of control. But that's how it is on big trips. Some going up, some going down, some going nowhere at all.

The next day I carried a double load as far as Camp II. The following day I climbed alone to Camp III where I found our tent peppered with holes. The Yugoslavs had done their best to repair it with duct tape but the wind still whistled through and spindrift had half filled the end nearest the door. As darkness fell I watched the two Yugoslavs returning from their high point. One of them descended immediately for Camp II while the other burrowed in with me. The next morning we arose early and jumared to the top of our lines carrying more rope, ice screws, carabiners, food, and a tent. It was a gray, lusterless day and we exchanged few words.

What do you say about a falling rock, anyway? About being cold? About how hungry you are and how you can't stand the thought of eating? About the lyric that keeps circulating through your mind every time you take a step? Or about the things you left undone at home and what a waste it is hauling gear up a face where all you are accomplishing is increasing the likelihood of getting yourself killed? Hours pass. Lungs ache. The tedium and fear tangle around each other like snakes. Then suddenly you are there and done with it, pounding in an ice screw, hanging your gear, and watching your partner descend. Time to pull on my parka before the cold can seep into my chest cavity. I swing my gaze over to the South Face of Lhotse and the South Col on Everest. There is an Australian expedition on Everest this season. How are they doing over there today? I wonder. Then it occurs to me that maybe they're looking this way and asking themselves the same thing. There is a tug and I look down. My partner is on the second rope now and it's my turn to start descending. Okay, come on, Childs. You know how to do this. Don't go unclipping anything until you've had a good look at it. Check everything twice. Let's see, all those gates screwed shut. Let's go...

By the time I reach the end of the ropes my partner is already heading downhill in the direction of Camp II while his countryman slowly makes his way toward me with another load. I gaze for a moment at the gathering storm then crawl inside the tent and get the stove started. When my companion arrives I pass him a cup of soup. We talk a little and he dumps his gear. He has just shaken off the snow and started to scramble through the door when the first rocks impact a few meters to our right. We both scream at the same time.

It was not the first time we had heard rocks go by. Nor was it the only time they had landed nearby. It was just that this time they were bigger—much bigger—and they were landing closer. We could hear them rattling down the slope above us, rumbling and crackling, then buzzing through the air like incoming artillery. A sound that grew like the last yamp at the end of light and life, and which ended in an explosion of snow and rock and ice. We dodged around inside the tent like mice, never knowing which rock would end it all for one or both of us, waiting and screaming. By the time it was over we were completely broken. Neither of us was willing to spend another night up there. Taking our chances with the climb was one thing, but neither of us wanted to die in our sleep. We were in the process of packing when a flake the size of a dinner plate tore through the roof of the tent, incised my companion's jacket like a scalpel, and buried itself 15 inches into the floor.

It took us all night to descend. The storm had grown teeth by then with strong winds and heavy snow. So having worked hard all day to get up the mountain, we worked hard all night to get down. Fortunately, my companion's wound was not serious—a deep bruise, perhaps, but no broken bones or bleeding—and though dazed and sore, he was moving stoically. We both lost track of time and place. The snow made it nearly impossible to communicate or figure out where we were. In the absence of any other science we simply let gravity take us down. I have no idea how long we struggled or how long the storm raged. I do know that sometime toward morning the wind quit and the sky turned the color of chlorine and we could hear voices. Then we spotted the yellow domes of Camp II's half-buried tents beneath 3 feet of new snow. The people inside were cooking breakfast. We went to the larger tent, which I unzipped and shoved my friend inside. In that instant I saw three faces: the other Yugoslav and two of the late arrivals. Then I closed the door, shoveled out the ruins of our supply tent, and crawled inside. It was cozy enough with plenty of food and fuel. The rest of the day I spent eating and sleeping and doing sit-ups to stay warm. I counted the squares in the rip-stop and thought a lot about Ovaltine. The next morning I heard voices but slept until noon, anyway. It was still snowing when I finally stuck my head out. The day didn't look to hold much promise but I was suddenly eager for companionship, so I loaded my arms with sausage, brown sugar, and tea and groveled my way to the big tent. Only the two Yugoslavs were inside. The fresh troops were gone. Down, not up. The Yugoslavs just shrugged their shoulders. This time we all knew that it was over.

By the time we finally made it back up to Camp III there was nothing left, anyway. An avalanche had swept it all away. Tent, gear, and dreams—all gone. We collected what we could, shoved our garbage into a bergschrund, and started home.

That was pretty much it. Over, up, down, and back. Neither success nor failure; just an experience from which each of us is free to take and leave what he or she may have learned. Just like life, as someone once said, only more so.

Was it worth it? Well, personally, I got a lot out of it. I saw some amazing scenery. I made some good friends. W...

have been better off on one of the ridges. Our disposition as a group was perhaps better suited to their elegant fluting and corniced architecture than the objective horrors of the West Face. Still, it was not so much the route as the timing that defeated us. We were simply there too soon. The West Face of Makalu belongs not just to climbers who are fitter, faster, and stronger than we were, but to a new generation. In the future some team of super-alpinists climbing without fixed lines or confused objectives, equipped with gear and eyes and ambitions that we just did not have, will climb the West Face of Makalu. They will come from the ranks of those to whom a new set of "last great problems" will fall until they, too, have consumed the possible and watch in amazement as what remains is redefined by their children. And in that age the West Face of Makalu, too, will be just another route, on just another mountain. And Lord I'd love to be there. Wouldn't you?

BLUE WATER BLUE

It is the sailors, who have been beaten and battered by the sea, and who have cursed and damned her, who are her true lovers.

—Isak Dinesen, *Winter's Tales*

␡

There is no mountaineering equivalent to the utter terror of being at sea in a storm. Twenty years of hard climbing had in no way prepared me for the autumnal gale that beset me and my 22-foot Drascombe lugger during a solo voyage on the outside of Vancouver Island. A quiet winter and several pleasant punts around the San Juan Islands had done little to assuage my memory of that truculent sea and howling wind. So, with less than seven days of vacation available, I decided to take my first sailing trip of the following season in protected waters. What I gave up in adventure I would reclaim in content by re-creating Peter Puget's voyage through the Sound that currently bears his name.

Mike Seeley's decision to join me gave my plans a much needed boost. The fact that Seeley had spent most of the previous two years rowing baggage rafts on the Rogue River made it possible for me to consider increasing the historical accuracy of our trip by leaving my outboard behind. Furthermore, he had saved my life two years earlier during a stormy bivouac on Mount Stuart and, thereby, confirmed my faith in his ability to make good judgments. These considerations added to the fact that he didn't snore or get seasick, knew how to read a chart, ate anything put in front of him, and possessed even less of a social life than me made him the perfect choice as first mate.

These details attended to, we raised sail early on the evening of July 3, wetting the Drascombe's hull in Budd Inlet, the southernmost point of Puget's voyage and our starting point. It was dead calm as we slipped away from the dock, and the sails were immediately dropped in favor of

Station under the command of Captain Vancouver. Keeping the miserable souls at his feet focused on their responsibilities must have seemed easy in comparison.

I cannot say the same for Seeley and me. By mid-morning of July 6

tidal pools. Late in the day a breeze arose out of the west, which enabled us to travel much of the length of Carr Inlet before putting the helm around and heading north for Filucy Bay. It was twilight when we dropped our hook and made our way ashore. In the last light of day we walked to the beach where Puget had spent his hardest night.

It was easy to imagine the scene: rain-soaked and bare-footed men huddled under the protection of the trees, a few crouched over the embers of a smoldering fire, the others peering into the darkness for intruders. A confrontation earlier in the day with a group of local Indians had left them on edge. According to the journal of Thomas Manby, a crewman of upper-class birth and a notorious liar, Puget's crew had been attacked by savages and forced to fight for their lives near this location. Dr. Menzies, however, records that only a passing crow was shot, and that Puget's concern was more based on the Indians' ignorance of his fire power than any threat to his life. Departing the beach, Seeley and I were happy to stop by the Longbranch General Store for ice cream and beer.

We spent another pleasant night on board and awoke to a clear and warm day. The sea, unfortunately, was flat as glass. We quickly hauled anchor and I rowed while Michael went about putting away the sleeping bags and firing up a pot of coffee. Much as Puget had felt the press of time toward the end of his voyage, so were we beginning to think about getting home in time for work on Monday. Not a breath of wind arose to

oars. Preferring to see no omen in this inauspicious beginning we laid to it good-naturedly and in less than an hour had fetched ourselves a northeasterly that soon had us, as Samuel Eliot Morison describes, "dancing before the wind with a bone in her teeth."

potato chips being opened.

Puget's start had been more heavily laden. Departing from his mother ship, the HMS Discovery, early on the drizzly morning of May 21, 1792, the young lieutenant found himself embarking on a voyage that was both ripe with possibility and rife with danger. Charged by Captain Vancouver with "exploring the bays, straits, and estuaries" to the south of what is now called Restoration Island, Puget bore the additional weight of knowing that these waters held the expedition's last best chance of unearthing a Northwest Passage to the Atlantic. Added to this was the fact that frequent glimpses of Salish and Sealth Indians provided an unknown peril. No contact had as yet been established with the local Indians, and Puget was uncertain as to how they would react to his intrusion.

Our consternation at a falling wind and another turn on the thwarts was mitigated by the fact that we were still making steady progress. While I can't say the Drascombe pulls easily, nor that Seeley and I were the match of the "six pig-tailed salts pulling at the long oars" in Puget's boat, we made good time up Case Inlet and were pleased to drop the hook somewhere around 10:30 P.M. in the lee of McMicken Island. Under the light of a full moon we put clams to the boil, rigged an awning between the sticks, rolled out our sleeping bags, and once more resorted to beer. All in all, a most promising commencement to our journey.

The following day bore similar portents. After breakfast and a brief walk around McMicken, we pushed off and spent just long enough at the oars to catch a breeze in mid-channel. Running wing-on-wing toward the small town of Allyn, Washington, we placed a fishing line over the stern and put our heels up. This area had been similarly kind to Puget. After three days of hard rowing and steady rain he had caught a breeze in Case Inlet that allowed his crew to finally stow their oars. Then, as the clouds parted and their sodden clothes began to smoke in the warming rays of the sun, the looming hulk of Mount Rainier suddenly appeared to the east. Archibald Menzies, ship's surgeon and a biologist, would later remember the moment as the most stirring of his thirty years at sea.

Docking at Allyn, Mike and I encountered an equally memorable sight. A bar occupies much of the Allyn wharf, and by the time we arrived the annual Fourth of July oyster bake had been running at full throttle for several hours. Crews from a dozen motor yachts crowded the wharf, some holding fishing poles in one hand and margaritas in the other, others lying like beached salmon on the rough tread of the dock, stomachs pink with sunburn and backs stained black from creosote. Blocking the front door of the tavern we found yet another sportsman who had fallen asleep holding his head over a bucket. Taking special care in stepping over him we made our way indoors to join a gang of yuppie Harley riders who were occupying the tables. Since neither Mike nor I were in the mood for screaming, smoking, or playing nonstop nostalgia rock on the jukebox, we were soon back at the boat.

Our return voyage was just as entertaining. The combination of good weather and a long holiday weekend had brought out what seemed to be every boat owner in the Northwest. For two hours the Drascombe bounced in the wake of an unbroken skein of power craft, all overladen with passengers and horsepower, and all of them cruising the Inlet like lost teenagers on a Saturday night. Cars honked at us from the shoreline, jets roared overhead, and every 50 feet along the beach vacationers gathered at barbecue pits to roast marshmallows, eat hot dogs, drink beer, and play their stereos at maximum volume.

In the midst of all this the afternoon breeze suddenly grew teeth and

it was with a double-reefed main that Seeley and I made a wet beat Stretch Island State Park. Using a pulley-buoy anchoring system, quickly transported our necessities ashore in preparation for a night the sand. Our years of guiding allowed us to rapidly assemble our cam make dinner, dispense yet another ration of alcohol, and lie down in o sleeping bags just as the first tinge of alpenglow began to bathe th western aspect of the North Cascades. At that very moment the skylin erupted with a cataclysm of skyrockets, cluster flares, roman candles and firecrackers. It was like a mini version of the end of the world. In every direction applause, cheers, the echoing of cherry bombs, and the screams of the wounded filled the night. Point detonations burst forth from every patch of beach and cobble. Sirens whined on distant roads and somewhere the descendent children of the displaced Native Americas of Puget Sound must have been laughing out loud.

The bombing of Dresden could not have involved more pyrotechnics. Still, the wreckage of dawn on Puget Sound was less than might have been expected. There was already movement among the dew-soaked bodies on the beach by the time Mike and I set off the following morning. The wind, however, was conspicuous in its absence. Our journey down the Nisqually Reach had us once more putting our backs into it as the sails luffed and the sun beat down upon our shoulders. Nevertheless, clever use of the local tide and current tables allowed us to make reasonable progress, and by nightfall we had anchored in Oro Bay, close to where Puget had spent his third night out. So benign was the evening that Mike and I slept without putting up our tarp. Puget, on the other hand, had brought his crew ashore under a punishing rain. Already chilled, they erected their tents, gathered firewood, and moved their supplies to land before partaking in a dinner of mold-ridden hardtack and grog. After that, guard duty was assigned and the remainder of the crew allowed to lie down upon the wet ground and sleep. It was the kind of work for which Puget was more than qualified. At twenty-eight, he had already been at sea for over half his life. His last two years prior to joining the crew of the *Discovery* had been spent in combat duty off Jamaica

help us in our efforts. Even worse, the tide turned and we soon found ourselves pulling vigorously at the oars simply to remain in place. Over the next several hours we watched in dismay as an elderly woman walking along the shore passed us like an Olympic sprinter. Later, a pair of sea kayakers appeared in the distance, stopped along the b-- lunch, napped, chatted

...... talents, they were certainly a ......use of mine. Stepping to the helm, I proposed that Mike continue to row while I gave closer scrutiny to the charts and winds. It seemed to me a logical course of action well in keeping with our Puget theme, yet I am sorry to report that my crew's response to this strategy was both sorely limited in historical perspective and tainted with a certain ugliness. I moved back to the oars.

As the day passed we took turns napping. Seeley curled onto the floorboards in front of the lazerette. I added a cushion to our rowing thwart in order to get a better effort from my legs. In fifteen minutes both my companion and my rear end were sound asleep. Sweat ran in a trickle down my spine. I counted strokes, boats, and birds and searched for imaginary creatures among the clouds. After half an hour of that I began a new game: this one involving trying to guess the true nature of the undulant reflections cast on the waters at either end of my oars, then raising my eyes to the object itself. A dock, a tower, a dog, a tree. And, at last, the Olympics. My climbing had always taken me east into the Cascades and I knew little about the parallel range on the other side of the Sound. Tales of alpine rain forest and moss-covered rock had always kept me away. I studied them with interest, then turned my gaze back to Rainier. The line of Liberty Ridge was clearly visible and I could recall with accuracy slogging to its summit in calf-deep corn. Never again, I murmured to myself and then thought that perhaps I had fallen into the habit of investing myself in things that require too little of me, that happen too fast. My life, like my climbing, had always trended toward technical difficulty and short-term commitments. Perhaps being an adult, like rowing this boat, had more to do with taking satisfaction in the long haul. Even the most wearisome of journeys, I was beginning to realize, reveals more about the traveler than it does the terrain.

Seven hours later, arms weary and crisp as french fries, we hauled the Drascombe out at Boston Harbor. After striking the masts and storing gear we sat down at a nearby picnic table and drank a final toast to our trip, vowing never again to overlook the usefulness of the internal combustion engine. After a full day of continuous rowing we had also decided that Puget's crew were made out of better stuff than we were. It is tempting to say the same thing about the body of water to which Puget bequeathed his name. Yet I have witnessed enough misery in my life to know that if the modern world carries with it certain afflictions, it also contains an equal number of appeals. It is hard to believe, for example, that Puget's crew would have turned down our Gore-Tex jackets, insulated underwear, canned beer, or Advil. And the Sound, despite everything that is wrong with it—its infuriating sprawl and industrial waste—remains a place of astonishing beauty. All that is required to save it is change, change that the tattooed salts accompanying Puget would have told us, begins with the will to do so.

CHORICHO

In the darkness before the dawn this mountain spoke my name...

—Author unknown

⌐

... naked feet, whispering and clustering in small groups before the cottage on the edge of the expedition field, crouching on calves like knotted mahogany and holding out their ancient hands to the fire where a young policeman was cooking *paratha*. Emaciated dogs pawed at the dirt near the tents of a French camera crew whose Mediterranean dreams went undisturbed by the guerrilla creep of ragged children who, like miniature Pandoras, were opening boxes in the dark and making off with Gallic tarps.

The Islamic vespers of night gave way to the *sotto voce* discourse of daylight. The citizens of dawn began loping along the pathway, clicking the loose stones beside our tent with their feet. Haji Fazil arrived wearing a black woolen cap, white trousers, and a cloth vest. The crowd waiting in front of the clay shack parted before him. A visit from Haji Fazil, *numbadar* of Askole, was considered a great honor. I limped on swollen feet to reach the flat-strapped bed frame on which he sat talking with Captain Jawed Shaukat, our liaison officer. We nodded to one another and drank white tea from cups still swirling with glacial sand. The glass tapped on the balsa scabs covering my lips and collecting in the shade of my nose. My stomach was humming and I felt dry as a peanut.

Jawed turned to me, gesturing toward Haji Fazil. "He says there are porters. Very good men. He will send them up this morning right away with a police officer." Haji Fazil smiled and I grinned back, holding my fingers self-consciously to cover my mouth. The old men gathered closer, nodding their heads and smiling.

"He says you have done a very fine climb," Jawed explained, beaming with parental pride. A square brown hand extended toward me from a white sleeve. Everyone grinned then. My lips split and I could taste blood sweet as maple syrup.

All the men in my family lived and died in the unions. Detroit is that kind of city. I've never thought back to it with affection, but the dichotomy of the assembly line—the division between those who owned it and those who worked it—sticks in the back of my mind, and it was with more than a small amount of discomfort that fifteen years later I found myself playing capitalist exploiter to the working class of the Braldu. But I mean we had a contract! Ian Wade and Jawed had sat out there in the heat of Bongla and written the whole thing out and the porters had all agreed to it. Yet every night as we sat down to eat came the dull eyes of need, the convenient misinterpretations and forgetting, the refusals.

Our head porter never seemed quite capable of resolving these things. Doubts hung around commitments and expectations like flies. He camped us where there was no water and carried no load. He frequently seemed more anxious about our poverty than the porters and asked often about the down parka he had decided we should supply him despite our assurances that we had no intention of having him carry above base camp. He waved off those explanations as if our, "alpine style" was a personal embarrassment.

We fired him in Askole. He hung around until the French Bridge where Will Miller forgot his patience. We had lost others along the way but there were always so many porters coming back from having carried for the French K2 expedition that we were able to hire replacements quickly. We asked Captain Shaukat if he wanted a cook since he would otherwise be alone once we went up on the mountain, but he only laughed and said no, he was quite capable of looking after himself. When the last porters disappeared back down into the valley and we were left alone to our mountain, our relief bordered on the ecstatic.

During the trek in we had met with the Uli Biaho group on their way out. It felt odd to meet them there, these fellow climbers—friends, but suntanned and done with it, headed home with their success. We

siuing, Payu.

We followed the trash of two earlier British expeditions up the icefall and set our advanced camp in a shallow cwm at 17,500 feet. Five days of up and down and a prolonged storm later, we sat stewing in our tents and listening to Mike Goff outside grumbling to himself and shoveling snow. Like Christmas in the suburbs. Only it was July and Mike was building an object, not creating an emptiness. When the noise stopped and we emerged, we found not an igloo but a monolith 8 feet high, perhaps 10 feet around, with frozen gear hanging snow-shrouded from it like laundry in Alaska. We laughed, and then later, when we'd eaten the last of our rations and the cold was once more driving us back into our tents, we tied our boots on loosely and walked counter-clockwise around the structure.

Down for more food and up for the climb. Three days later I sat on a twilight ledge warm as a sheep and partner to a dozen gargoyle flakes while high above, Ian struggled on verglassed rock and gully ice the consistency of cold porridge. The rope moved in sporadic leaps. Discs and pebbles skittered past, but no Ian. Somewhere on high he was bridging among the inky silhouettes on the edge of a second great ice field. My attention drifted easily away from climbing to contemplation of a horizon where Nanga Parbat and Rakaposhi carved pyramids of white out of the darkness.

In time there came a muffled call. It was Ian, descending on rappel, purple and yellow, illuminating the night. He huffed heavily, as one will do at such elevations, and sat beside me. A bit below, Will and Mike had supper on the brew and our bivy tents dug into the wall of a crevasse. We spoke of having come far that day and stood to make ready for the long traverse home. As Ian leaned forward I noted a rusted ice ax dangling from a harness.

And what here, sir? I asked, pointing a mitten.

He'd discovered it sticking out of the snow on a small ledge, brought to it by a peculiar British sensitivity for relics of defeat. We hemmed a while about what sort of retreat they must have suffered that had them leaving ice axes behind with 1,800 feet of ice and 3 miles of glacier to go. We had accumulated an anthropologic dossier of shame in the traces they had left of their messy capitulation: ice gear, runners and clothing, tent poles, syringes, discarded food containers, and mounds of assorted garbage pocked their withdrawal like Elphinston's retreat from Kabul. Such is the onus of big-team expeditioning, and we were anxious to ascend from their high point on the wings of the new religion.

The southwest face turned out to be as edgeless as space. No place to rest our weary ankles and those heavy packs constantly wanting to pull us backwards, accentuating any diagonal lunge into a near pirouette. And very exposed. But never a leader fall and always working upward without the tattletale colors of fixed rope behind us. Thirty feet above where we had been we were trackless as muggers in a Manhattan night.

Lousy place after dark, though. We never really found a proper spot to sleep on the whole face. Ian and Will ended up dangling their feet from dull, if pragmatic, ice shelves while Mike and I manufactured inventive disasters. Our art form reached its zenith at One Bun Bivy (20,700 feet), where we both spent the night hanging batlike in our Lowe packs thinking unclean thoughts about the ladies who do the stitching.

The following morning a falling canteen provided graphic testimony as to just how high we were. So impressed were our teammates that Will quickly demonstrated his enthusiasm for the line by blocking a pumpkin-sized rock with his jaw and Ian froze to candle wax the tips of three fingers leading onto the long-sought west ridge.

The mountain changed there from Karakoram spire to Himalayan

had brushed the picket heads of Tartary with orange shadow.

Being cheerful, good-natured lads and up by 2:30 A.M., we had better to expect of our mountain than the vexations of that summit day. Not a trace of the walk-up had we seen from the glacier. Bergschrunds and cotton candy. Mike at last shuffled like a crab on a concave plane around and up and over a bit of overhanging froth placing us on a long, steep ice field. Metronomes set at 21,500 feet, we climbed voiceless and unprotected into an azure sky. Too tired to think of beauty, we thought instead of nothing. Plodding last in line, I watched hopefully as Mike mantled with the ease of youth onto the highest cornice in view. Will shouted down something about having further to go, but I put that out of mind as the oxygen-starved ravings of a mad man. That deceit enabled me to join the others on the cornice but it did not give us the top.

One hundred feet across a rotten horizontal mustache of feeble snow rose another cornice, perhaps 20 feet higher than our own. Despite my suggestion that it only "seemed" higher owing to angle and altitude, the others were not deterred. Mike worked out to a granitic breast and returned. Since I was second in the afternoon queue, it was then my turn. Fortunately it was the sort of thing I do best: dull and straightforward, more shoveling than climbing, stopping here and there to catch my breath and once to drop partially through a Buhl hole, then crawling on hands and knees to a point where at last going on meant going down.

I ran through the regular list, counting Trango towers, trying to re-member which was Gasherbrum and which was Mashberbrum, wondering if we could see Hidden Peak. K2 and the Pakistani route on Payu stood out. I forgot most everything else. Just the normal touristy photographs and a couple of aspirin dropped in the hole my ice ax had left on top. So much said for super-alpinism.

The rappelling was horrid but done efficiently. Never even a close call. We were back in base camp in three days, and since my former military training tends to give me a look of susceptibility when volun-teers are called for, 'twas I who left at 5:00 the following morning with Jawed to send back porters and call for transport from Dasso.

Just as well, I might add. For while my companions were opening a can of tomato sauce that would have them all lying on their sides and writhing with food poisoning, I was swimming in a sulfur hot spring and eating vegetable stew beneath an apricot tree, the Paul Revere of the Braldu.

MOUNTAIN OF MAGIC, VALLEY OF MARVELS

Logic which meant not logic as a system applicable to

I

There is another groan from inside the transmission, metal shredding like paper this time, pieces just falling away. Blind mechanical agony when I try to take the thing anywhere but into neutral. The beast is dying on me, coasting gearless at 5 miles an hour with no more than maybe 150 left in it. To get where? A small blue-and-white sign on the side of the road says TOUET. Touet? On the map it is a dot without a name, a bend in the road that in real life curves away from a 2-foot-high stone retaining wall on the edge of eternity. There are clouds down there playing earth. God knows how far you'd have to fall beneath them to get to the real thing. At 3 miles an hour I move closer to the center of the road. On the inside edge of the curve is a granite *paroi* scraped smooth by cars and trucks keeping away from the brink. There is also another sign, same size and lettering but with a thin red diagonal line running through the name, which means you are leaving town, picking up speed for the 35-mile downhill into Nice, where an hour ago the sun was shining and people were outside in shirtsleeves drinking *menthe a l'eau* and talking about taking a weekend trip to Corsica or Italy.

But that is the other side of the road.

Touet, whether you are coming or going, is not the kind of place that leaves much of an impression on visitors. Tucked neatly within the walls of a small canyon the village faces north, away from the sun, and is not, therefore, a *montagnard* community in the strict sense of the word. Its buildings, both private and public, are drab and humorless, and the people of Touet seem to spend a lot of time with their hands in their pockets leaning against things. Yet it is not the kind of place where people talk a lot about leaving. Those who feel that way left in September with the young people and the tourists. The rest stay on as if sentenced to it by their migrating Italian ancestors who just never got further than this along the Col. Whatever it was they were running from or toward, it stopped interesting them here. They put down their bags and built themselves a town hanging off the cliff in a poor man's cantilever out over the abyss.

It has probably been a long time since anything as exciting as my visit has happened on a New Year's Day in Touet. It seems to turn out most of the townspeople. The women come slowly wearing wool scarves and dirty cloth aprons and stand at a respectable distance in a loose semicircle behind their men, who have walked up a little closer. Close enough to look over my arms and into the vitals of the engine. Nobody says anything. Not much to say, I guess. Gray hair under dark blue berets gets scratched. Ashes fall off the ends of yellow-skinned, hand-rolled cigarettes. Stomachs hiss behind pinned together vests. But there's no Touetian tradition for saying howdy to a stranger. Interest grows as I begin removing the air filter. The man who should be mayor comes over and takes a position of authority between the headlights. He is wearing a small hammer-and-sickle pin stuck through the material of his coat just above his lapel threads. I sense that the fire of revolution still burns bright within him. *"C'est dommage,"* he states with satisfaction. And I think, Funny, me and my dying car, symbols of the capitalist economy, way out here in the middle of nowhere. A woman who is younger and better dressed than the others approaches and stands off to one side. Her posture is that of a boxer. Touet's exile, I think to myself. A sordid story in those eyes if ever I have seen one. Perhaps an affair with the village priest? He has given her the widest circle. Worse things have happened. In France even the men of God are existentialists. You can see it in their faces as

not so filled with optimism about the car's chances.

"It is an old car," he says after about a minute and a half under the hood. "Fixing it is probably not worth what it will cost in repairs."

Memory and impulse tell me to believe him. In the three years that I have been abusing it, the Simca has crossed the Alps more times than it has had its oil changed. He and I nod as if we understand each other, shrug our shoulders, look at the engine and shake our heads, then engage in a variety of murmurs and sighs.

"I can give it a good home," he tells me with a faint smile.

I do not like the idea of just abandoning the thing in Touet. I owe the Simca more than that. I try and explain this to the mechanic, and he seems to understand. He will tow it into Sospel if I want him to. It is downhill most of the way, he says, and he has a friend there who might be interested in buying it for parts. I still have a peripheral hope of reaching St. Dalmas by nightfall.

II

Towing the car downhill does not turn out to be as easy as I had for some reason imagined it would be. The road drops sharply, wobbling and twisting back and forth across the face of a steep hillside. The Simca wobbles and twists behind us. All this squealing and tilting does not seem to affect the mechanic. He has been here before, hauling bigger loads than mine. He takes the bends down-shifting, tapping the brake with the toe of his Adidas, folding the two cars into a neat V, and then lining them back out again for the straightaway leading into the next right-angle turn.

We have dropped below the level of the rain clouds and into a light mist. The valley appears like a soggy yellow and brown quilt. Vineyards have been hand cut out of the mountain along its sides, shoveled level and propped up with field stones in long undulating terraces. Piles of brush and weeds have been left at the ends of every other row for spring burning. Olive trees grow in gnarled single-line groves along the road. Further down we pass gray farmhouses with gray barns and red brick tile roofs in need of repair. Cattle graze in the yards. Small flocks of poultry peck at the dirt. Hand tools lean against stone walls. But nowhere are there any cars or TV antennae. The mechanic shakes his head. He does not understand farmers, he says. As far back as anyone can remember his family has farmed on Madagascar. Since the day he was old enough to start thinking for himself it seemed to him that a man's hands were meant for something besides raising calluses. "I never understood any of them," he laughs. "They never understood me." He came to Sospel a few years ago for a friend's funeral. He was offered a job working at the garage and has never gone back. Not even to pick up his belongings and say farewell.

It seems we were both soldiers in Vietnam. Different armies, but the same war, more or less. Not a hell of a lot had changed there in the fifteen years since we were there: same people getting pushed around and abused, watching their homes go up in smoke, not getting much to eat, getting shot at, bombed on, and screwed over. We shrug and mur-mur again and leave it at that. He asks about climbing. Hooking my car to his truck he had seen the gear in the back seat, left there after a week on the sea cliffs around Toulon. He has done some scrambling, he says, but never anything serious enough for ropes. He is intrigued by all the chocks and carabiners. Time goes very quickly after that. I tell him about the peak I have come here to climb and he says, yes, he knows it well and has even been up as far as the canyon to have a look at the drawings.

He has friends, though, good friends, who go up and climb the buttress routes almost every weekend in the summer. But not now, not with all the snow? He lifts "snow" into the interrogative. His way of asking why I am doing my climbing alone and in the middle of winter. I tell him about the way things keep piling up in Grenoble, about grabbing at free

isn't the time to be going up into the hills. But I am here now and as long as I have come this far I might as well go the rest of the way. This talk takes us to the edge of town. We have already agreed he will take me directly to the station and do what he can for the Simca later. If it is beyond repair, I tell him, I will give him 15 percent of whatever he can get for it. This seems to please him very much. We shake hands on it at the bus station and he leaves without even mentioning towing fees. I watch him pull off with the Simca rolling behind, wave, then turn and go into the terminal. The bus to Bringue is about a beer away from departure.

III

It is a well-known fact that all the buses in France are new except for the ones in Paris, which are old, with hand-worn wooden bancs, roll-down windows, and standing room in the back where you can put down a suitcase or a rucksack filled with three days' food, a stove, a change of clothing, a *pied d'elephant*, a down jacket, 165 feet of rope, several carabiners, a couple of ice pitons, and pair of crampons, with an ice ax tied on the back. There is, of course, no such room on the new buses that go between the towns and the mountains. This is all part of the Plan. The driver of the bus I am now riding was very insistent about the Plan and, at one point, became rather ugly about demanding that my rucksack ride in the underbelly compartment like all other personal baggage, despite the fact there were only three other citizens on his bus, all three of whom were holding their personal baggage on their laps. This, too, is part of the Plan, as no plan would be a plan without exceptions. But today I am in no mood for such dickering. Today, where I go, my rucksack will go. To all his officious bellowing I simply shrug my shoulders and murmur, "*Je ne comprends pas,*" the ultimate gambit of any stranger in a strange land. This leaves him with only the option of physical force which, given the difference in our size, he elects to ignore (a behavior universally recognized as endgame). I ride in peace with my arm around my pack and the two of us watch the scenery go by. Farms mostly, and old men in worn-out suits standing beside empty mailboxes with their hands in their pockets, watching back. The road is a lane and a half in a nonstop, 20-mile S-curve upon which the driver has elected to carry out his revenge upon me. The beer I had inhaled in Sospel rises to the back of my throat on every corner. As we approach Bringue, where my ticket runs out, I transfer to the train. There is a forty-five-minute wait for the train at an empty station. I look through the postcards and settle on a Paul Tiarrz photograph of climbers in the Vallée Blanche. I scratch out a few words to an old friend who is working as a lawyer in New York. Postcards like this are meant to impress upon him that I made the wiser of career choices, though neither of us could ever inhabit the other's life, anyway. I drop it in the mail and step outside to look for a urinal. Naturally, the public facilities are closed and I wind up in the park behind a statue dedicated to Bringue's war dead. A woman with two children walks by and scowls at me. It is hard to imagine this day could get any longer.

IV

Taking the train into St. Dalmas is like riding the Lionel Line in a department store window at Christmas. St. Dalmas is like a toy town: Grimm Brothers' houses stand in crooked two- and three-story rows, their painted shutters and polished mahogany doors bearing brass name plates and cast iron knockers in the shapes of lions and eagles and women's hands. The roofs are one-sided red brick tiles with cigar-box chimneys. Vaulted corridors lead one street to the next. Children just returning from school in Tende chase each other over the cobblestone roadways, screaming and throwing snowballs.

stacked up and piled to one side of the veranda. The driveway and parking lot have not been plowed. There are lights on in the bar, the kitchen, the downstairs living quarters, and one of the rooms on the second floor. Everything else rests in suspended animation, awaiting the return of summer. In town I was told that "Georges" is the name of both father and son. Although young Georges bought out his father a long time ago, the old man, who lives in Narbonne with his wife, his dogs, and his asthma, still makes a once-a-month pilgrimage to St. Dalmas to have a look around and see how his son is running things. He is never pleased, never stays for more than a day or two, and has never stopped paying the bills. That's what I love about France. Ask a question and you get the answer. The old man is a pain in the ass, I was told, but his son has no head for business. Fortunately, he married well and between his wife and his father the bills get paid. Such is life.

"Young" Georges, I discover when I meet him, is a tall, heavy-chested man, probably once very handsome but now running downhill fast on the steep slope of his mid-sixties. There are deep lines around his eyes and his mouth has the downward cast of many disappointments. It is my impression that when business is down Georges spends most of his time at his bar with a few old friends drinking. I can't blame him: the bar is a perfect place for it—the walls are a celebration of better times. Of dreams that once hovered close but never quite came to be. Except here, of course. Pictures are better than real life anyway, and here there are hundreds of them. The Mountain from a dozen different angles; sheep, trees, and flowers; the cave drawings and literally scores of fading black-and-off white photographs—of climbers with their arms draped over one another's shoulders, squinting and grinning, wearing baggy plus fours, stocking caps, and hobnailed boots and leaning on chest-high, thin-handled ice axes. Sections of rope hang on chamois horns and someone has gone to the considerable trouble of welding a pair of old five-pound steel crampons into a bar lamp with Georges's name engraved on a small plaque at the bottom. Above the bar mirror is a large oil painting of Georges as a young man standing on the summit of the Matterhorn. He has a rope tied around his waist and there is a storm gathering in the distance. Slumped against the bar, Georges is almost unidentifiable as the young man in the painting. Life has extracted a steep price from him for his family's generosity with his debts.

The oldest of his friends, a hoary, used-up coat hanger of a man with teeth like a mouthful of brown shells and wearing broken horn-rimmed glasses, is first to notice I have entered the room. He comes over carrying his right arm up against his chest like a medal. He presents the hand to me for inspection. Half of it is missing. Three fingers, a twisted thumb—just enough to hold a cigarette. He is a small-town horror and sees me as a mark from The City. In Kathmandu an act like that would get maybe half a sideways glance on a good day. I nod my head in appreciation and he goes limping back to his friends.

Georges tells me to have a drink while he has his wife fix up a room. He pours a glass of good Bordeaux and leaves. I am thoroughly enjoying it, in spite of the four old farts watching me, before one of them finally asks the inevitable question of all travelers. "What country are you from?" Since it has been a long day and I am here to climb, not to defend the Marshall Plan, I tell him Sweden. His face falls a little. Seems as though he doesn't know much about Sweden. Just that we (they) have a king. But America, he knows all about America. They blew off half his friend's hand here, didn't they?

"Did you know that 40 percent of the people in New York City are *drogues*," he states, not really asking.

I try and look astonished and tell him no, I thought the number was closer to 80 percent. My escalation takes him by surprise. He does not like being put in a position of defending the enemy.

running water, a deep feather mattress with a half dozen blankets and quilts on it, and a window facing the Mountain, which is visible now as an opaque outline against the gathering darkness and salmon-tinged clouds. I wash, change into some clean underwear, and eat supper downstairs. Georges and I talk about my plans as he hustles back and forth from the kitchen. He says that there will be a lot of new snow, but that the trail as far as the canyon is well marked and I should be able to follow it without difficulty to the hut. After dessert he brings out maps, some old photographs, and a bottle of cognac. We wind up sitting there talking until well after midnight. He tells me about the Mountain's geology, about the climbing and the drawings. About how he had made his first ascent of the Mountain when he was fifteen and by the time he was sixteen had done all the routes on the buttress worth doing, including half a dozen firsts on the overhanging wall. His parents sent him to a trade school in Digne to learn metalwork, but his heart was at home and in being a guide. After his apprenticeship and his twenty-first birthday that is what he became. He worked out of the hotel, meeting his clients in this same room before there were any pictures on the walls. Some of the people that came were climbers but most were not. There were archaeologists and artists, naturalists and writers, or businessmen on holiday. He would pack all the food with good wine and clean sheets for the straw mattresses in the refuge. Usually they would stay up for two nights.

The first day he would take them around the canyon and point things out. Then, on the second day they would either climb or he would hike with them up to places where they could take pictures. At night he would do the cooking and the washing, and afterwards they would sit out on the porch and he would smoke his pipe and talk about the Mountain, or himself, or the weather, or whatever they wished. If it was a young couple he would slip discreetly out the door and go sleep under the stars. They were all fine, intelligent, appreciative people in those days, he says. Once, during the war, two young German soldiers hired him. They were on leave and wanted to do the northeast face. It was a very difficult route and they spent two bivouacs on the Mountain together. The third night they slept in the refuge. When they went back down and the boys put on their uniforms he felt very sad for them. It was as if he was sending off his own sons to war, and he made them promise to write and come back. Neither one ever did. Other than that, he saw nothing of the war. It worked no hardship on him. Not until after it was over. Then, for a long time, no one came. And when they did return, the tourists who came to his *auberge* were a new generation. Whatever had gone on out there, whatever he had missed, it had changed them and made them hard. They no longer wanted guides or picnic lunches. They wanted to do everything themselves. Nor did they want his box-camera postcards any more. Depressed and penniless, he married a woman five years his senior who bought him his father's *auberge* and ordered him to quit climbing. He agreed and dedicated himself full time to becoming an innkeeper. That was more than twenty years ago and since that time he has never been up the canyon once. "I used to tell myself that I would make one last climb before I died," he explains wistfully, "but not any more. Now there is only this," he sighs, gesturing to the room.

VI

In the morning a little before 6:00 there is a knock at the door and the smell of breakfast. A tray has been placed on the chair beside my bed with *café au lait*, two croissants, and the keys to the refuge. It is raining when I leave, and despite the coffee I feel cold and groggy and angry with myself for not having gotten to bed earlier. The trail is muddy and difficult for its lack of anything to step on. The rain falls harder and then, a 1,000 feet uphill, turns into snow. I am beginning to experience a real sense of regret at not having stayed in Aix with my friends. As I stop

it lacks the blood magic that Jewish mothers have spent their whole lives putting into their chicken soup. By adding a little milk, a little butter, and a few well-chosen spices, the aroma is gratifying, anyway. Cooking it, stirring and tasting it, and playing around with the stove takes my mind off the ghosts and memories that have followed me up this mountain. Soup is the liquid equivalent of having someone to talk to. From what other people who travel by themselves write, I have the impression that my demons are not unique. Each of us, I suspect, has our own little Hitchcock buried somewhere inside our heads. Sitting in this cave is an open invitation to all kinds of memories I have tried hard to forget so I busy myself with some minor housekeeping. Things like putting away the stove and digging out my mittens. But the gremlins seem to go with the natural decor of the cave and it is with more than a little relief that I regain the upward inclination of the trail.

I can see that in the summer the canyon could be a mysterious and, in its own way, beautiful place. But in January it is just another alley for the wind to funnel through, crusting and drifting the snow and glazing everything with ice. Perhaps a kilometer further up the canyon I come to another cave. A larger one and a good place to get out of the wind. In the frozen stench of God knows how many generations of man and animal who have squatted in here out of the wind and pissed against the wall, I find my first rock painting. The figures are at about waist high and protected by a horizontal lip of rock. Someone has painted a picture of what looks like a kind of five-legged antelope running right to left. Beside it is the just barely visible outline of a man. Maybe the Hunter. Perhaps someone important in those days. Important enough that the artist figured people would always remember him, so he didn't put down his name. Or maybe this is his name. Either way, he and the artist and their people, the place where they came from, and the way they lived have all been lost. Stories told and forgotten, new ones told and those too forgotten, all in the same way that in another 15,000 years, despite all our efforts to the contrary, we too will be disremembered.

VII

Not much has been answered about these drawings. Not enough to get in my way of imagining some hirsute impressionist crouched in front of the wall working by torchlight with paint made from mastodon blood, sketching in the outlines, holding the brush between his fingers like a pencil, making up for lack of skill with broad strokes of imagination. Maybe he was a priest and the work is a symbol, a sacrifice, a sign. Or maybe he was just a man with an unwholesome affection for animals. The only thing we really know is that whoever did the drawing came here to do just that—to draw—and nothing more. No other artifacts have ever been found here to suggest that anyone lived in the valley. No pottery or tools or skeletons. The cave is certainly not what you would choose for a fulltime dwelling. It only works as a canvas. A place for drawings. A placard upon which a man came a very long way to tell the world something of importance which, all this time later, is still there and nobody understands. The questions go unanswered and the drawings are left to deteriorate on their own. Well, not exactly on their own. Not in this case. Someone has taken what looks to have been the pick end of an ice ax and scratched the French equivalent of "fuck you" across the bottom.

Not that that kind of wantonness comes as much of a surprise. A little mindless destruction doesn't shock anybody anymore. In fact, it almost comes as a fulfillment. That satisfying shake of the head. The gratifying condemnation of greed and selfishness that so offends. That pleasing emphasis on the word "them" and all their transgressions.

don't know about these drawings, etching the

what

very act that

Not so very long ago I worked with a group of talented people on an educational film series about the sad state of a famous North American river. For our big exposé we rented some canoes and paddled out along the shore one night to where a factory secretly gushed waste into the water. We were there with our clackboards, stun-guns, and Arri BLs at 3:30 in the morning when all the nasty glop the owner said he wasn't dumping came spewing out of his pipes. We recorded the whole thing at twenty-four frames per second. When we showed it to the factory owner his response was to laugh. He thanked us. He was losing money keeping the factory open. Trying to put his business into compliance would bury him financially. The only reason he kept the thing going was to keep people employed. The hell with it, he told us. You win. I'd rather retire to my condominium in Key Biscayne, anyway.

So much for all our glib liberalism. We saved a few scrod and put a couple hundred people out of work. The hard-liners among us stayed to finish the project, determined to never again come face to face with the "other side" of an issue, while the rest of us dropped out and decided to find some other way of making a living. Except me. I left and came here to the same kind of paradox.

Apparently there are some people besides old Georges who care about the Mountain and its drawings and what happens to them. A few are well-placed politicians and other influence wielders within the French government. But nothing continues to be done. The reason lies in a very clear-cut division of interests. The "intellectuals" (a word that somehow seems less pretentious in French), who include a lot of people who at one time or another have climbed the Mountain to look at the drawings, are in favor of having the sections removed from the canyon and placed in various museums for safekeeping, study, and display. Georges along with other local shop owners and politicos take the position that the proper historical and economic solution (after all, they are French) is to leave the drawings in place. The feeling in St. Dalmas is that if it were not for the cave drawings no one would come to visit the area, which means hard times and angry voters. A situation that requires a skilled political response. Appropriately, the central government in far-away Paris seems very unlikely to do anything. Citing the challenges of these complex economic times it is almost certain that they will not surrender the funds adequate to restore or relocate the drawings. As on the road to Touet, safety is in taking the inside edge.

From my point of view, I believe that the drawings do, for better or worse, belong to the Mountain. Too much has already been put away to protect it from the people it is being protected for. Take these drawings out of the darkness and stench and cold and the cave, and they become just another academic curiosity. They have lost their reality, their place in the world. If they are destroyed where they stand...well, that is of value, too. We should have to look at each other's dirty work. It is the only purely objective means we have of seeing ourselves in perspective. Lock everything of value up in cages and you have saved a picture of what we were at the cost of seeing what we are now. Better to have the truth right out there in the open where you can't help but be a little embarrassed about it, and perhaps angry enough to start doing something.

The two hours I had spent sitting in the cave writing notes and staring at the wall have put me behind schedule. The trail is getting dark and I am getting apprehensive about arriving at the refuge on time. There won't be anyone there waiting for me, but it is good to keep to schedules. They are something to think about when I am walking.

VIII

...~xceptionally fine refuge. Sleep comes easily, as does drag-

...It gives me a chance to look around

...flashlight. The

...

ancient pot-bellied stov... ..

lamps hanging from pegs and nails and a chand.....

of a wagon wheel. Out front is a porch overlooking the canyon and in back an outhouse and lean-to for firewood. The caretaker has nailed a cigar box to the wall and left a note asking for donations for the wood-cutter. I drop in a few francs and listen to them make contact with other people's money. Those same former tenants have left condiments, powdered soups, a stack of magazines in several languages, and a very respectable selection of half-consumed bottles of wine. I can see that this would be a very easy place to stay for a few days with some close friends or maybe two German boys running away from the war. It all reinforces a long-held admiration of mine for the Alpine hut system. A few months earlier I had climbed to the Refuge de Vallot on the Chamonix side of Mont Blanc and found it open and half filled with snow. Someone had kicked in the door and made a fire in the middle of the room from strips of wood pried off the windowsills. They had caved in a wall with their ice axes and left a corner full of turds. It is a function, a friend of mine says, of the numbers. The percentage of jerks always stays the same. It is just that with so many more people in the mountains there are so many more jerks. Thankfully, I am the only jerk in this refuge today, and I have no intent of doing injury to anything other than my own lassitude.

The signs seem good for climbing. The weather is marginal, but holding. I am feeling more rested than I have since leaving Grenoble two weeks ago. I am well fed and warm and there is not a single gremlin in my head. Before leaving I divide my belongings into the essentials that will be going up with me and the nonessentials that I will pick up on my way back down. While sorting through my goods I discover that water has somehow gotten inside my camera. I wrap it in a plastic bag and place it with the other items to be left behind. What's to take pictures of anyway? A camera tells worse lies than words.

I walk out and lock the door behind me. I wonder who I am locking out. Then I hang the key on a nail under the eaves. Anybody who has made the trek this far deserves entry. And, besides, I would not object to company about now.

IX

It is snowing harder than before and in more of a semicongealed kind of sog than yesterday's thumbnail-sized flakes. It splats on the rocks and soaks through my anorak down to my long underwear in just a few minutes. But I am into the rhythm now, moving quickly and easily over gritty holds. I am very warm and very content to be where I am, doing what I am doing. As the route moves to the northeast the wind picks up considerably. It makes me more prudent about holds and thoughtful of *verglas*. About halfway through the only hard section the slush turns to pea-sized hailstones. At the top of the pitch it takes me twenty minutes to bring my hands back to life and at least another ten blowing into my mittens to get my fingers working well enough to put on my crampons. The next section is an easy couloir, but it is very exposed at the bottom and I keep close to the side, using holds on the rocks where I can find them. Halfway up I am afflicted by doubt. I should say here that I do not particularly care for what goes on inside my head when climbing very exposed ice gullies alone and unroped in a hailstorm. There is no one to perform for. Too many variables. Too many reasons to doubt. I am not a loner by choice, but by circumstance. Six hundred feet and I am nearing the top. A rightward traverse onto rock. A cloud banks itself on the Mountain as if it intends to stay and it becomes hard to see beyond the

gray walls looming immediately above me. I cannot see a logical exit
...d a platform on which I wait nearly an hour for the mist
...course, other than that the murk grows
...r down. I dig a shallow
...side, at-

make ...
am done with dinner. ...
hours or so, nothing to do but to try ...

X

Sleep does not amount to much. Lying on my side in the prenatal
position, my hands under my head, I spend most of the night thinking
about what will happen if the weather is the same—or worse—in the
morning. Thankfully, the hail stops and there is little in the way of wind.
I try to imagine that the chill I feel is symptomatic of a clearing sky
though the rock above me hides any possibility of confirming that. I
dodge any temptation to indulge in philosophical reflections. I experience no poetry. Toward morning I find myself thinking about an article
I had read in the *International Herald Tribune* about other climbers.

It seems as if there is the group of people who have decided after some
intense Bible study that old Noah did indeed first step ashore after that long
and celebrated rain upon the slopes of Mount Ararat. It is, therefore, their
plan to organize an ascent aimed at looking for pieces of that remarkable
boat. They would very much like to find any remains of the Ark and
bring them down to prove to the world that, yes, it all transpired just the
way the Good Book says it did. I think they may be missing the point.
Religion is faith. Proof dispels faith. The search for physical proof to
a question of faith better represents doubt than devoutness. It would be
a shame to see them coming down from the mountain with the Ark in
their rucksacks, knowing that it would wind up in some museum in the
outskirts of Nashville where you would be charged $10 to have the

existence of God confirmed by some nineteen-year-old tour guide with a fake smile and a Farrah Fawcett hairstyle. Faith depends on a willingness to accept mystery, not the desire to seek corroboration. Finding the ark would only succeed in making an auto repair manual out of what is already a great book. It is very much the same with this climb. I am here to find the line between faith and proof. Starting a route is faith, finishing it is proof. This ledge is where those two planes meet. A rope would only separate me from the outcome. I know what I can do, and I know that this route is within my ability. Even on a windy and snowy day I know that I have the skill and experience necessary to solve whatever problems lay ahead. I just don't know if I have the faith. Tucked deep inside my bivy sack I toss back and forth in my search for evidence that will deliver the outcome I desire.

It is a fool's crusade. The very point of big questions is that they have no answer. No certain outcomes. They challenge us to make choices based on 80 percent of the information. To roll the dice on a hunch, to test our faith. My guess is that the Biblical enthusiasts climbing Mount Ararat will come down with something less than proof absolute, something more than empty-handed. The skeptics and the true believers will all look at the same evidence and take refuge in the fact that it confirms their opposite perspectives. Causes do that to people. They help us rationalize our experience in this world by qualifying everything in terms of capital and country, the search for beauty and method, conquest and technology, and, sometimes, the search for God. Excuses that the first climber probably dragged with him up his mountain when the very point of going was for no other reason than just to do it. But the world wants to hear more than a sigh so he gave them religion. Books of stone. Funny how little things change. Restless and cold to the quick, I wrap my arms around demon doubt and light the stove.

XI

The weather outlasts me. By morning the hail has turned to a steady drizzle. I pack my gear and traverse across the shelf to where an easy step brings me to the ridge and an agreeable descent. Finishing the climb would mean another night in the canyon, and by now I am anxious to ̲ ̲ ̲ down. I have what I came to the Mountain to get. I reach the ̲ ̲ ̲ coffee and dry out. I throw the rest of ̲ ̲ ̲ a good

floorboards. I eat in ̲ ̲ ̲ just as well. I haven't got anything to tell him. ̲ ̲ ̲ rucksack beside me, with another driver taking out his vengeance on the road. My friend the mechanic is at the station when I arrive…in the Simca! Turns out his friend didn't want it after all. It should get me as far as Grenoble, he says, but he is making no promises. Touching the car I tell him that it's all right, that this time things will be different. The mechanic nods his head. He then tells me what he wants for his troubles. His price is considerably more than I had expected to pay for repairs plus towing. I whine a little, but the amount we settle on is closer to his number than mine. He buys me an espresso with a rum chaser for the road. We talk for a while and he seems honestly interested in what I have to say about the Mountain. I wind up getting back into the car feeling a lot less angry about what it cost me than I probably should have.

Just before dark I cruise into Touet. The restaurant is open for dinner and my stomach is willing, but the rest of me just does not respond. I ease into third gear and put Touet in my rearview mirror, leaving it where I found it—in the shadows and on the edge of the abyss.

PART III
People and Profiles

DANNY BOY[3]

Fleeing from short-haired mad executives.
The sad and useless faces round my home,
Upon the mountains of my fear I climb;
Above, a breakneck scorching rock; no caves,
No col, no water. With excuses concocted,
Soon on a lower alp I fall and pant,
Cooling my weariness in faults that flaunt
A life which they have stolen and perfected.
—W.H. Auden, *Two Climbs*

Dear Bob,

These are my words about Dan. Well, mine and Auden's. No one can express sorrow better than the poets. I will write Cindy a long letter after we go over to the coast. We're planning to hike up the beach, throw some flowers into the ocean, and say a few words over the place where Dan died. Hopefully, our small commemoration will coincide with yours.

I keep asking myself how one person could touch so many lives so quickly, so easily, and then just go? Fall comes early here and the leaves are already turning yellow down along the river. The wind hisses through the pines at night and the weather is wet and cool. Time to gather ourselves together for winter. Diane says she had gotten in the habit of looking out the kitchen window in the morning wondering when we'd see Dan's truck parked under the trees, tailgate down and the blue foot of his sleeping bag wet with dew. Toby had been waiting to trade tree frogs with him. Pete, our neighbor, had been hoping Dan would work with him on the house he's building. Even the guys from the Saturday afternoon soccer-and-beer club keep asking when he's coming back. Never is never easy to explain.

Twenty-five years of climbing have given me the best moments in my life and left me a short list of friends taken too early. Avalanche, falls, cold—gone so fast last words were never exchanged. Illness, I think, is more humane. It lets you say goodbye. It lets the family summon their courage, it allows for plans. But those things are for us, the ones who get

stoked a small fire, dried our wrinkled feet, and talked

you talk about in front of a fire—the things we loved, the things we wanted, the things we had. It's a funny balance, this division between satisfaction and hunger. Dan talked about good things behind—his family, his friends, sailing and soccer—and the good things ahead. It was typical of him. No judgment, no expectations, just a supreme grasp of the moment. The next morning when we shouldered our packs and looked back up at the wall, both of us feeling beat up and exhausted, it was the mountain that interested Dan, not our route. That's the kind of guy he was. Everything in proportion.

I can't think of much else to add. They say that to every moment there is a beginning and an end, an alpha and an omega. A first and last. Dan was one of the few people I have ever met who could see both. I will miss him very much.

With much affection,
Geof

---

[3] *Eulogy for Danny Sefahrt, September 24, 1997*

THE DREAM TEAM

You maintain a shifting distance between yourself and your job.
There's a self-conscious space, a sense of formal play
that is sort of arrested panic...
                                    —Dan DeLillo, *Underworld*

We were the dream team. The perfect pentagon. Five guys who couldn't miss.

We first met at a party hosted by a mutual friend. It was one of those dress-like-you-live-in-Manhattan things with everybody wearing black. Our acquaintance's way of saying thank you to all the little people who had made him so incredibly rich, not to mention a convenient way for him to write off a few thousand extra bucks at the end of the fiscal year. This particular event was held in a warehouse near the waterfront. I could tell it was hip because a very large woman with pink dreadlocks and very bad teeth met my wife and I at the door and provided us with henna tattoos. Inside, an Industrial Zouk band called Napalm Beach played to a room full of software designers gyrating beneath a chrome-and-chicken wire *porte cochere* while around the edges of the dance floor scores of date-less yuppies clustered at long buffet tables steeped in postmodern *poo-poos* and designer beers. As is our habit, my wife headed for the bathroom; I went looking for a drink.

I am not quite clear on what happened next. Maybe it was the fact that I was feeling out of my element. Or maybe it was the kid with the eyebrow rings pouring vodka martinis so stiff they peeled the enamel off your teeth. Maybe I was just hungry. I don't know. But for one reason or another I found myself standing with a group of guys eating a plate of stolen *hors d'oeuvres* and talking about the stuff you talk about at a really hip party when you've shown up wearing wing tips, a pinstriped gray suit, and a paisley tie. We were not complete strangers. I recognized most of them as friends of friends, faces to nod to in a crowd, names I'd heard over cocktails though none of us, as it turned out, had ever actu-ally been introduced. Yet from the very beginning our conversation had

unusual. Ripe with the kind

ery wild exaggeration had be
time ago.

Nothing could have been further from the truth. Short, tall, long-haired, short-haired, and crew-cut, we were an amalgam of contrasting styles and unlikely confederation. Our professions, politics, and predilections were diverse. So much so that the only thing we really held in common was the fact that business had been good to us. Yet the longer we talked and the more we drank the clearer it became that in some cool, funny, who-really-gives-a-flying-fuck office party kind of a way the robust cynicism of our public persona was the smugness of a lie. Our successes had come at the cost of omissions and compromise that, ultimately, had made minions of us all. We may have been big dogs, but none of us was a lead dog. We were part of the pack. Supernumeraries in a world of such greed and stupidity that intelligence profited one less than blunt arrogance. While the platoons of investment bankers and federal attorneys surrounding us moshed at the free food, we railed against the injustice of it all and laid the groundwork of a new economic paradigm.

We would call this new organizational concept "an enterprise of businesspeople" and upon that principle we would build a partnership of equals. A firm too lean for dishonesty, too energetic for fear, and too freewheeling to smother the creative gifts of even its most obdurate wage earner. Before the night was half over we had already churned through a roll-out plan and billed our first 1,200 hours of virtual consulting. It was the most fun I had had at a party since college. I was still buzzing when my wife poured me into the car.

"You know," I told her on the way home, "we should get a better car."

Two days later the gates to Volvoland swung open for real. "There's someone on the phone for you," my secretary told me over the intercom. "It sounds important."

It was. It was the host of our party. He wanted to get the five of us together again, for dinner. "Nothing big," he said. "I'd just like to talk with you guys about your venture."

"What 'venture'?" my wife wanted to know when I called.

"Oh, it's nothing," I reassured her. "Just an idea I've been working on with some other guys."

"You aren't going to quit your job or anything, are you?" she wanted to know.

"No, no. It's nothing like that," I lied. "It's just dinner."

We arrived wearing game faces and doublebreasted suits. We nodded and shook hands. No one smiled. We ordered drinks, made small talk and watched the Celtics lose to L. A. on the television. The fact that we were about to listen to a pitch on a business that had existed for two hours at the bottom of a bottle of vodka never came up.

Our host arrived smiling. He was wearing a pressed flannel shirt, Patagonia slacks, and a pair of $300 Cole-Haan loafers. When he sat down we leaned toward him in five different postures of approval. It must have been the easiest sale he'd ever made.

"Use my company as a lab," he offered. "I'll make it worth your while."

We ran the numbers on a cocktail napkin the moment he left. The accountant among us nodded his head. "Even if we lowball outside sales for the next two years," he shrugged, "we're talking about hitting the ground with a half million in commissions."

In truth, it looked better than that. Too good. We'd all seen sure things go up in flames before, so our communal inclination was to move slowly. Yet the fact was that with a median age of forty-five and enough missed opportunities stored in our collective memories to fill a hard drive with regret we all knew that this was our last best shot. Nobody else was standing in line waving money at us. This was it. The yin and the yang. So we went through the numbers again. We argued out every "what if" imaginable, speculated on the collapse of a variety of industries, and

We were presold and

sketched out a client list,

ment where we could stay when we were in the city. Dinner, dessert, and dozens of drinks later we sat in a miasma of cigar smoke and testosterone telling Clinton jokes and making stupid promises. It was one of the headiest moments in my life. I felt cool and utterly stoked. Cocky, self-certain, and scared absolutely witless. Something I had not felt in a very long time.

Reduced to its fundamentals, business is—for lack of a better word— well, *boring*. Most things simply happen too slowly to elicit very much excitement. Even those bet-the-company moments you read about in *Fortune* take place in an atmosphere so laden with technical, financial, political, and regulatory encumbrances that almost no one is even aware that they have taken place. All the decisions that mean anything are made by default. Choices that no one chooses. So remote is management from the actual work of the organization that by the time its policies reach the people who have to carry them out they rarely generate anything more than confusion. Confusion that fans the flames of fear; fear that turns even the most aggressive companies into bureaucratic gulags; gulags that turn into game parks where survival is more politic than purposeful, where all perspectives are short term, and where talent is treated more like a threat than an asset.

By far, the most dramatic thing that happens in a business is the bloodletting. Take re-engineering, for example. Now here is a concept in which the same grossly over-compensated executives who have allowed the company to become slow, bloated, and unresponsive launch cost-cutting initiatives aimed at eviscerating production staff in order to inflate stock prices and thereby enrich themselves despite the fact of their responsibility for the problem in the first place. These pogroms arrive at the frontline like a reign of terror in which divisions are pitted against divisions, people against people, job against job. The result is, of course, a workplace where being misunderstood, undervalued, or over-estimated constitute a ticket to oblivion.

It is a world in which it is easy to lose clear sight of yourself. A game of delayed dreams and minor lies. A world which, for twenty-five years, I had kept in balance by climbing.

I cannot say that this balance was achieved by intent. In fact, for the first ten years of my working life it was my jobs that supported my climbing—not the other way around. Penniless and uninsured, shifting residences with the season, I lived for much of my early adulthood on a diet of brown rice and adrenaline, taking jobs only when I had to and madly pursuing a checklist of crazed ambitions. The vexations and misery that plagued the rest of the world passed me unnoticed. The wars and recession of the 1970s and the expensive gas and cheap political theatrics of the 1980s were background noise. Pitching my tent wherever desire placed me, I lived happily outside of civil society in a mini-universe of high endeavor and questionable outcome. Death was near. Life was rich and every day was ripe with new possibility.

By the mid-1980s, however, I had begun to feel the need to put down some roots. The road is both a seductive temptress and a hard mistress. After a decade on the bum I was tired. It was time to discipline my wanderlust. To wake up under a roof instead of a sun-faded nylon ceiling. For lack of any other option I went back to graduate school. Thereafter came a succession of jobs that gave me the time and money to expand my range as a climber even as they reduced my number of days in the mountains. I trained harder and got out less. I slept in a bed more than a sleeping bag. I got married and had a child. I moved up in the world. Time went by.

And then one day I woke up and realized it had been a year since

ˮ ˄lˑˑhˑ were; I didn't know if I

manding of my soul and a ˑˑˑˑˑ

But if I had abandoned climbing, climbing had not abandoned me. As I walked out of the restaurant that night and stood on the curb, the sense of epiphany that welled up inside me was familiar. I had been in that place before—standing in etriers, leaning my weight into the void, searching for a way up or a way out, blinded by desire and bound to my partners by covenants of perlon and steel. Though I now stood in a black wool coat leaning into a breeze that blustered dust up Beacon Street I knew I was teetering at a similar point of decision. The choice between safety and what Kipling called "the wildest dreams of Kew." I had come into that restaurant with a good job, a supportive boss, and a solid retirement package. Now I stood with my back to it all facing into the abyss. And everything inside me said jump.

⌁

My secretary cried when I gave notice. My boss and I shook hands. We mumbled platitudes about arranging an orderly transition. Then I cleaned out my desk and went home. By lunch I had ordered a computer, a phone, a fax, and an answering machine. Before dinner I had hired an accountant, rented an apartment, and put together a newsletter. That night the five of us held our first conference call. We qualified clients, sketched out the draft of a brochure, and did some budgeting. We talked about different ways of dealing with the distance, delegating the workload, and sorting out our roles. It bothered me that we hadn't done a better job of defining what our majority investor meant by "operating on a high-speed learning curve," but I didn't want to be the first one to blink. This was a time for raising hopes, not for indulging in doubts. It was like ascending a fixed line. You just have to put the questions away, shut down the arguments raging inside your head. Strung out in the void is a poor time to be contemplating the probabilities of frayed sheaths, creaky pegs, or the lack of conviction in your partners' eyes. Once the line is weighted it is time to be thinking about what you are doing, not why.

—

Karl Marx noted that when a worker takes a job he transfers not just his labor but the whole of his life to his company. That's how it was for me, anyway. What my wife thought to be obsession I rationalized as nothing more than commitment. The truth of the matter was that the promise of wealth had reshaped my moral geography. I was consumed with the arithmetic of my ambitions. One-eighth of every dollar we earned belonged to me. Everything else in life shrunk to those proportions. All of us were pushing, searching for the mark that was going to make us millionaires. I went to work at 6:30 A.M. and stayed there until 10 P.M. I was on the road constantly. I bought a cell phone and made cold calls from taxis and street corners. The few nights I made it home I spent in front of the laptop typing proposals, reviewing the numbers, reconfiguring the five-sided features of our expertise. Once a month we did dinner—mini-galas at which, with our ties loosened and suspenders hanging from our waists like slingshots, we argued over plans and strategies, laughing, and filling page after page of flip-chart paper with our roles and goals and Magic Marker matrixes.

But as the months went by our beneficiary became more involved. The thread between his desire and our directions grew frayed and knotted. We found ourselves talking less and listening more, scribbling notes on pieces of torn fax paper, leaning back in bleary-eyed exhaustion, and nodding our heads to impossible commitments. It was like carrying a rock in deep water. Little by little the weight of doubt dragged us down. But no one said anything. The morphology of our self-deception was that simple.

Which is not to say we didn't have our glory days. In the beginning, ... showed up in the trades. Im-

tion, but I cut down ...

off their sides, and started climbing there three or four days a week. By midsummer my chalk marks inscribed routes on every surface not buried in leaves. I felt fit and strong. In September, with our business falling into chaos, I called an old partner and arranged a trip to Yosemite.

We arrived after midnight. I had made a pitch in Silicon Valley that afternoon and I was still wearing my suit when we drove past the darkened ranger booth. It was my fifth visit to the Valley, my first in almost fifteen years. We had packed a tent but scored a last-minute cancellation at the Ahwanee Hotel. Thus ensconced, we arose to warm croissants, took box lunches with us to the crags, and repaired in the evenings to the terrace where we smoked Cohibas and drank lite beer.

We stayed for two weeks. On the last day of our visit my partner expressed his interest in touring the boulders of Camp 4. We climbed listlessly and spent most of our time drinking tea and eating cookies in the parking lot. I pointed to the 30-foot-by-30-foot field of hard dirt where I had spent three full summers in the 1970s, a site even the bears had avoided for its wretchedness. It was now occupied by a group of Japanese students who were sitting at the picnic table where I had once performed drunken ollies onto upturned beer bottles.

"It's really not much like it used to be," I told my friend.

"Nothing is," he replied in a tone that said it was me and not the world that had changed.

I will not go into the details of our failed IPO, nor the contracts that never came due, nor the numbing realization that, regardless of what it cost, our benefactor had absolutely no intention whatsoever of letting us take a spanner to the mechanism of his wealth. There are no victims in this story. We were full participants in our own demise.

People tried to tell us it wasn't working. Our wives. Friends. Colleagues in the industry. We chose not to listen to them. I didn't figure it out until one of our benefactor's senior vice presidents told me. We were in the Canadian Rockies together and I could tell he had something on his mind. We had picked our way up a long mixed route under a looming cornice and had walked less than 50 feet away from the summit when the cornice collapsed and scoured our route. The descent was just as bad. We wound down through barrier after barrier of seracs creaking with instability. It rained and snowed and rained again. Rocks whistled past our helmets and I could feel my partner slowly beginning to dissolve. By the time we reached the glacier he had tears in his eyes.

"We can't go back there," he said.

"We don't have to," I told him. "We'll head over toward Calgary. We can go do some rock climbing on the east side until the weather clears up."

"No," he said, "I don't mean that. I mean back to work. We can't go back there."

A blind man could have seen what was coming next. My climbing companion got the chop first. I got the news about a month later. It came through an intermediary, a friend of a friend. A face to nod to in a crowd. It was all very high-minded, of course. Lots of handshaking and blame-taking. I got a great going-away party, a photo album, and some time to prepare. It was more than I expected and all I needed.

Of the guys I left behind, all were gone within sixty days. Two stayed for a month—both in much diminished posts—then bailed out for better offers. A third went on full commission (an in-house euphemism used to denote financial exile), and the fourth was fired outright. He sued, of course, but didn't win enough in court to buy him back much satisfac-

we will be able to make a ...
other days we are happy for the good ones.

I would be dishonest to say I don't have regrets. I am sorry for having put my family through so much turmoil. I am regretful for having behaved as if covering the angles was the same as solving the equation. But most of all I am sorry for having gone so long without climbing. I get out one or two afternoons a week these days. Usually with friends who are about my age. Sometimes we fire it up and surprise ourselves. Sometimes we get to the crag and wind up standing there alongside the road, drinking beer and just talking. Either way, the focus it has brought back into my life astounds me.

I agree with those who say that climbing is not life. It is much better than that. In climbing you get nothing other than what you absolutely deserve. It has no skin color, no gender, no rules that matter, and no lawyers, referees, or pushy parents. You can't get any more or any less out of climbing than exactly what you put into it. There are no dead ends in climbing, no barriers other than the ones we impose upon ourselves. The blend of skill, boldness, and desire that each route requires is unique unto itself and yet connected to every other route as if within one long and contiguous passage. Life is hard on dreams, harder on dreamers. Climbing was built for them. For in climbing success and failure both lead to the same place, to new resolves and new possibilities. Life should be so good.

The groundwork of our ruin lay not in the team but in the dream. Not in us, but in our vanity. Our goals weren't about anything that added up to more than money, and the fact is, they didn't even belong to us. We bought them and nodded our heads as if they meant more than they did. In the end the only way we knew how to give them a moral dimension was to make them politic. We out-placed blame the same way we out-placed our accounting. As if somehow the human heart has a bottom line. In climbing there are no middlemen to blame, no agency of ascent other than to take each step or make each move on your own. Dreams and desire meld, and no one other than you can fulfill your smallest longing. Our boozy chimera we sold too cheaply, too easily, and too soon to the wrong person. And then we waited for him to make it come true, never realizing that our dream was not his until it was too late. Or, in my case, just in time.

BIRD

When the terrain borders on controlled hysteria,
management of the unfettered imagination

Everybody has a j....

sometime in the late 1960s. Bridwell and fellow Yosemite lifer Jim Madsen have driven up to Glacier Point and are engaged in a bit of pharmaceutically enhanced eco-tourism when a tourist approaches with his poodle. The dog snaps at Madsen's ankles and Bridwell remarks to the owner that he should put his pet on a leash. Disgusted at having to share the view with two such obvious degenerates, the owner refuses. The dog snarls again. Madsen boots it over the edge.

"OK," Bridwell tells the dog's horror-struck owner, "you don't have to."

Whether your sensitivities let you laugh at that story, or whether the story is even true—and Bridwell insists that it is not—is immaterial. What is important is the tale. The strongest ties we have in climbing are our myths: the fables spun from parking lot to bar, from one crag to another, from climber to climber until the details are so convoluted and confused that all that remains is the telling. The written word can't capture what it really means to climb. The things that happen on rock are simply too visceral, too complex and personal to lay down on a page. The best climbing stories are the ones told out loud. And no one has had more stories told about him than Jim Bridwell.

The Bridwell legend is, of course, a caricature. Only slowly does the iconoclast whose dry wit, supreme talent, and incurable wild streak that forever changed North American climbing come into view. Part genius, part rowdy, the real Jim Bridwell is a pastiche of contradictions, both more and less than the sum of his tales. At fifty-four he is soft-spoken and reflective, still fit, and percolating with plans. He is wary of interviews. Celebrity, he knows, is a double-edged sword: an opportunity wrapped in heavy strands of adoration and vilification. Getting to know him, like climbing a wall, is a long and complicated process.

I first ran into Jim Bridwell in 1975. It was a heady time for both of us. I had just climbed the Regular Northwest Face on Half Dome in a methodical two and a half days. Bridwell, partnered with John Long and Billy Westbay, had made the first one-day ascent of El Cap's Nose, and was preparing to tackle the vast and uncharted real estate to the left of the North America Wall, a stretch that under Bridwell's tutelage would usher in modern-day big-wall climbing and be known as the *Pacific Ocean Wall*. I was quietly stealing a shower at the Curry Company employees' compound when the front door exploded open. "Bridwell's here!" someone shouted. Naked and soap-covered, I stepped out to have a look. On either side of the door stood a small group of sun-buffed minions. In the middle was Bridwell. He was leaning over the sink washing his face. He looked gigantic. Dusty-blond hair hung to his shoulders. The muscles on his back looked as if they were cut from stone. He was dirty enough to merit a shower, and perhaps just a little uncomfortable with all the fuss.

He is still uncomfortable with all the fuss. Reputation, he will tell you, is more important than recognition, and despite having one of the best-known names in American mountaineering, he is happy to move through crowds unacknowledged. Called a visionary by climbers as diverse as Royal Robbins and Jared Ogden, he is perhaps more gamesman than shaman. Like all great athletes, Bridwell's contributions to mountaineering have stemmed from a profound understanding of the game. He feels its currents and flow almost intuitively.

Midway through his fourth decade of hard climbing, Bridwell is still focused on the next step, which he says is "technical climbing at altitude." With little urging he will produce a photo of some Himalayan or Patagonian or Alaskan wall and trace a line where his route will go. He knows every challenge by heart. "We will climb this in the dark," he says pointing to a couloir. "This is where the big-wall section begins." At an age when most of his peers have settled down to career paths and pension plans, Bridwell is still hungry, still driven to make a statement.

He is probably the only one who thinks he has to. For most of us,

From the mid-1960s until the late

Long, "you have to understand that the accomplishments of the genera-tion that preceded us were mythical. We thought of guys like Robbins and Chouinard as icons. But Bridwell told us there were no myths—there were just rock climbs. And Bridwell was no icon."

Indeed, as the heroic figures of Yosemite's Golden Age were abandoning the stage, it was Bridwell—wearing purple bell-bottoms, a paisley vest, and a tatty bandanna—who stepped up and showed the world that anything was possible, if you had enough courage. Bridwell widened the definition of "Yosemite style" to encompass everything that went into building a life around climbing. In his glory days you could feel his presence in Camp 4 like a jolt of electricity.

Jim Bridwell may not have invented the low-ride, but anybody who has been in Yosemite and pushed his or her personal limits, stolen food off a tourist's tray, offended public decency, got drunk at their picnic table, played out their stay on crackers and relish, or slithered onto a half-driven piton 2,000 feet above the barbecued air of El Cap Meadow has stood along the banks of the river Bridwell and wondered at his beauty.

Not that the waters have always run sweet and clear. Away from the cliffs and mountains, Bridwell has backwashed into eddies of failed schemes and indifferences. The stubbornness and why-not attitude that have served him so well on walls have hobbled him on the horizontal.

Yet, as the current crop of young climbers goes out into the world to put up their own masterpieces, they do so in a landscape shaped by Bridwell's imagination. The Nose in a day, the Pacific Ocean Wall and Sea of Dreams, his ascents of Cerro Torre, Pumori, and Moose's Tooth were more than just routes, they were strides into the unknown that have inspired the brightest stars of a generation and left in their wake an unrivaled legacy of brilliant style.

To Bridwell, adventure is style. His obsession with minimizing bolts, for example, is less about ethics than playing dice with the limits of possibility. He can be a stern taskmaster but, says Billy Westbay, "He was always pushing us to be our best."

But as with all great achievements, there has been a cost attached.

"People don't look at me and say, 'My, how normal you look,' " Bridwell has said. "You know why? Too many lines on my face! From too many days looking up into the sun, or over my shoulder at the storm clouds—of being terrified. But you have to deprive yourself to learn, to move ahead."

The deprivation is, at times, much more apparent than the learning. Strands of gray infiltrate his still dusty-blond hair. His gaze is less penetrating, wearier than it once was. The line of his shoulders has been stooped by years of carrying heavy packs and hauling loads. Shaking hands with Bridwell is like picking up the roots of an old tree. His skin is hard and taut. His expression is frequently that of vague distraction, a look that turns easily to anger. He is not glib. He does not hold disparate thoughts in mind easily, and the halting, off-track associations that spike his conversation, like the weathered texture of his face, are legendary. As with so many of the myths and rumors that surround him, the description "head of a seventy-year-old, body of a twenty-five-year-old, and attitude of an eleven-year-old" captures his appearance at the cost of understanding the content of his soul. Impatient and demanding, a man of towering ambition, Bridwell has never let hubris rob him of his ability to view mountaineering within the greater context of life. A father, a husband, a pirate, and a pioneer, he has dreamed big dreams and made them happen. He has rolled the dice and had them come up sevens. The stories, as rich as they are, only tell half the truth. When in the 1970s

you could do it. When we looked up we saw granite. Bridwell looked up and saw the future. Then he went out, threw himself headlong at the impossible, and in so doing rewrote the history of climbing.

James Dennis Bridwell was born on July 29, 1944, in San Antonio, Texas. His father, Donald, was a war hero and an officer in the Army Air Corps. Like all military families, the Bridwells moved often. So often, in fact, that by the time Jim entered middle school he could more easily list the states he had not lived in than the ones he had.

Reclusive by nature, Jim spent much of his childhood alone, working on projects, playing with his toys, or exploring the woods. Later, as sports began to occupy a greater percentage of his time, he seemed to grow out of himself a little. A natural athlete, he excelled at everything and had it not been for yet another family move, Jim might have spent the 1970s dishing up split-finger fastballs for some triple-A farm team instead of putting up hard aid routes in the Valley. But arriving as a freshman at San Mateo High School in California, he discovered that the teams had already been chosen. Once again on the outside, he drifted away from sports and into falconry.

"I must have been a pretty strange kid," Bridwell laughs, thinking back to those days. "I was always hanging out in the woods, hiding in blinds and reading books."

One of those books was a guide to the national parks. Under the title "Yosemite National Park" Bridwell found a two-page photograph of El Capitan. Even at age seventeen he was tantalized by its immense scale. A few weeks later he came across another article—this one of an ascent of the Fisher Tower's Titan featuring photographs of Layton Kor. "That was it, man!" Bridwell remembers thinking. "I was already climbing cliffs to capture birds. I figured, hell, I can do that, too."

The next day Bridwell and his buddies were rappelling dirt mounds on a manila rope stolen from a transmission tower. Recognizing the limitations of this setup, Bridwell soon enrolled in a Sierra Club basic climbing course. "I was pretty good at it right away," he concedes. "But what I liked best about climbing was that I was accepted as myself." As his skills grew, however, he realized that his instructors "were not the serious guys I had read about in *Freedom of the Hills.*" The real climbers, he knew, were in Yosemite.

A superb middle-distance runner, Bridwell was offered a track scholarship to Purdue University. He turned it down in order to follow his high school track coach to San Jose State. He enrolled intending to graduate, but climbing was already exerting an increasingly powerful attraction over him. During the summer of his freshman year he made his first trip to Yosemite Valley. By the time he returned his interest in formal education was at an end. Bridwell lasted just four semesters. In the spring of 1964 he quit school and left for the Valley. "Hell," he explains, "I had important climbs to do."

Pitching his tent beneath the pines—not far from the location he would later make famous as the "rescue site"—the nineteen-year-old Bridwell looked around and took his bearings. Everything seemed inordinately rich and infinitely better than he ever could have imagined.

With Royal Robbins in Europe and Yvon Chouinard in the army, the reigning god of Camp 4 in the early 1960s was Frank Sacherer. "When I first arrived in Yosemite," Bridwell says, "there was no guidebook and no information. The only protection was pitons. Climbing was dangerous and people played it cautiously." Everyone, that is, except for Sacherer, who was insanely bold and emphasized a minimum of gear and a maximum of commitment.

Bridwell's natural athleticism and youthful boldness brought him immediate attention, and it took him just two weeks to elbow his way into the inner circle's pecking order. Jim Baldwin, a well-liked Canadian,

the fact that pushing the limits meant stepping over the line, holding nothing in reserve. Tormented and intense, Sacherer asked just as much from his partners as he did himself. He pushed and bullied, turning free time into workout sessions and meals into rewards. By the end of his second season Bridwell had accompanied Sacherer on the first ascents of Ahab (5.10a) and the Crack of Doom (5.10d) as well as the first free ascent of a Yosemite Grade V—the North Buttress of Middle Cathedral (5.10a).

According to Bridwell, when Frank Sacherer left Yosemite in 1966 to take a job in Europe as a physicist, "He had free climbed routes that the best climbers of the day said couldn't be done free. He had climbed routes in a day they said could not be climbed in a day. In the 1960s, Sacherer did more to advance free climbing as we know it today than any other single person."

Partnered by period luminaries such as Mark Clemens, Peter Haan, Jim Pettigrew, Kim Schmitz, Madsen, and others, Bridwell now set about putting Sacherer's philosophy into practice. Relying on pitons hand forged by Yvon Chouinard in the Camp 4 parking lot and Austrian kletterschues, Bridwell and his cohorts practiced a ground-up ethic that outlawed previewing, hang-dogging, or resting on gear. Even short routes were ventures into the unknown. Of that period, Bridwell's ascents of Outer Limits (5.10c), Catchy (5.10d), Wheat Thin (5.10c), New Dimensions (5.11a), Butterfingers (5.11a), and the Nabisco Wall (5.11a) remain his greatest works.

By the summer of 1967 Bridwell had become one of the Valley's best known habitués. Spending his winters in Tahoe where he worked as a ski instructor, he was invariably among the first climbers to return to the Valley in spring and among the last to leave in fall. It is an indication of the high regard in which his climbing ability was held that the park service placed him in charge of organizing and managing their high-angle rescue team. It was a move that would change the Valley's social structure forever.

Described by Doug Robinson as "the most trampled and dusty, probably the noisiest, and certainly the least habitable of all Yosemite campgrounds," the Sunnyside walk-in site—known to climbers as Camp 4—was the home of every climber who entered the park. Figures as diverse as John Salathé and Don Whillans had rolled out their sleeping bags on its hallowed ground. Dungy and loud, Camp 4 probably generated more stories per square foot than any of the vertical real estate surrounding it. Handing control of its choicest sites over to Bridwell, a future park superintendent would later confess, was "not the wisest policy decision we ever made."

Neither was it the worst. Lost amid the skewed tales of wild times and "living as one with the dirt" is the fact that Bridwell and his hand-picked gang of rescue technicians actually took their duties seriously. Rappelling off the summit of El Cap to pluck an injured climber off a ledge and deposit him safely on the ground posed technical and logistical problems no one had ever grappled with before. Over the next ten years the confederation of park personnel and climbers that formed Yosemite Search and Rescue (YOSAR) laid the foundation for today's high-angle search and rescue techniques.

On the domestic front, it is probably not too big a stretch of the imagination to suggest that Bridwell also found in Camp 4 the neighborhood he had never known as a child. Like him, its eccentric retinue of loners and misfits had escaped the suburbanized wasteland and aching loneliness of middle-class America to throw up their sun-faded tents and live, as Doug Robinson so perfectly phrased it, "like hobos in a paradise of stone." Now, with the keys to the asylum in hand, Bridwell moved quickly to create the city of his dreams.

Peopling the rescue site with the cream of Yosemite climbers, Bridwell and his chosen few lived as beggar kings beneath the great sweep of the Sierra in a New Jerusalem of golden light and endless days. Secure from

Then, as now, days began with the dregs of any available liquid left over from the night before and a spoonful of whatever remained in the pot. By 8:30 A.M. the more industrious residents of Camp 4 would walk across the street to the cafeteria. Half coherent and with sticks and leaves clinging to their hair, they would then forage the abandoned foodstuffs of horrified tourists until security, satiation, or disappointment sent them home to engage in the perpetual discussion of routes, partners, gear, and weather. Optimists worked on their dilapidated cars, the intellectuals read Ginsberg and Ferlinghetti, folk music drifted in the breeze, and by 5 P.M. the secret expeditions to new routes were old news. It was the perfect idyll.

Outside the Valley, however, another revolution was taking place. The values that had stood one generation through depression and war were being tossed away. Riots, assassinations, and the insanity of Vietnam were rattling the streets. Everything was upside down. Authority was in retreat while psychedelics, free love, and social agitation were everywhere. Everywhere, that is, but Camp 4. A situation that was destined to be short-lived. After all, the climbers of Camp 4 were already leading a socially unacceptable lifestyle, it only led to reason that the drugs and free love could not be far behind. And when they arrived, "The Bird," as he was now called, was ready.

"Almost every climber I knew used drugs," says Bridwell of those days. "We didn't use them on routes. It wasn't like that. We were using hallucinogens to help us understand what we were experiencing from a point of view seldom visited by the western mind. We were trying to make sense of this new awareness. To unfold the mysteries. Drugs were equipment."

It was a difficult adjustment for the old guard. Their crew-cut and orderly world was gone. The momentum was changing. In Camp 4 the beat poetry, mountain Chablis, and bongos of the 1950s had been replaced by Mararishi Yoga, blotter acid, and fuzzy riffs on cheap guitars. Yvon Chouinard, Royal Robbins, Warren Harding, and their cohorts had set a high standard. But although their final statements—the Muir Wall, North American Wall, and the Wall of Early Morning Light—were grand gestures, when the end of the Golden Age came it was marked by petty disputes, chopped bolts, and personal vendettas. A gilded era was gone and, as Bridwell puts it, "the Gods were bitter in their demise."

By the time the 1970s dawned Camp 4 was a changed place. The dulcet good life was gone. Now it was louder, funkier, and much more crowded. Though the summers were still reasonably peaceful, spring and fall brought hordes of long-haired outsiders seeking to imprint themselves on the walls. The scent of Camp 4's wood smoke mingled with that of pot. The midnight intrusions of bears foraging for leftovers were drowned out by arguments over chalk and passive protection. Coming to the Valley in those days was like going to church in a bad part of town. Climbers went there knowing about the gods and of their patron saints—Herbert, Frost, Roper, Pratt, and Kor—but it was the renegade that everyone wanted to emulate. Bridwell. Outsiders were happy to engage in the rumor-mongering and self-justification of life on the lower rungs of the social ladder. Tales of Bridwellian misconduct, arrogance, and daring were favorite topics around dinner. Deprecated and envied, Bridwell was Dean of Camp 4, and Lord of all he surveyed.

John Long arrived in Yosemite in 1971 with Bridwell in mind. Brash and muscular, toting an impressive résumé and carrying a chip on his shoulder the size of the Columbia boulder, Long pulled in and headed straight for the rescue site.

"I went to Yosemite dead set on proving something," says Long. "I wanted to be part of the cutting-edge group. I wanted to climb with the best climbers in the world, to push the world standard. That meant climb-

Bridwell again picked up the pace, training and climbing harder than ever. Soon the rescue site and its environs teemed with talented young climbers—John Bachar, Ron Kauk, Werner Braun, Mike Graham, John Yablonski, and many others. Wild and unfettered, they took to the rock like iguanas during the day and happily indulged themselves in the raucous parties and loose living of Camp 4 by night. There was no longer any philosophical agenda to getting stoned. It was recreation, pure and simple. One more way of expanding the high that was life in Yosemite.

"There were neighbors, love affairs, slums, parties, gymnasiums, loonies, territorial disputes, degeneration, and inspiration," Kevin Worral, a frequent partner of Bridwell's, says of those days. There was the Mountain Bar for scrounging drinks, the fireplace lounge for sitting out storms, and, if you were quick enough, free showers or a plate of purloined leftovers at Curry Village. "There was just nothing like it," says Billy Westbay. "There was this incredible energy. Everybody feeding off each other. It was an untouchable growth period."

As the energy increased so did the output. Bridwell's 1973 article for *Mountain* magazine entitled "Brave New World" stoked the fires even higher. Extolling the techniques and standards of Valley climbing, Bridwell's words excited climbers from around the world to come to Yosemite and test themselves in its granite crucible. With visitors from Japan, Italy, France, Korea, England, and Spain all elbowing their way onto the walls, a hybrid of new ideas and bold one-upmanship infused the Valley.

"Everything in the 1970s was open-ended," says John Long. "All of us believed Bridwell's credo that anything was possible."

EBs, tape, chalk, tincture of Benzoin, and nuts accelerated the pace of change. It was as if a veil had fallen. As if everything was up for grabs. The possibilities were mind-boggling and nobody understood them better than "the man." Playing minister and mayor, New Age Sacherer and old-age Ahab to this motley parliament of Ishmaelites, Bridwell set out to push the envelope. Where walls were concerned, the more he climbed the more he saw what was out there. And how vulnerable it was. Like the generation before him, Bridwell understood that any place on Yosemite's undulant granite was reachable if one was willing to spend enough time with drill in hand. An example needed to be set of what could be achieved by minimizing bolts and maximizing the adventure. Finding the line to best express that credo was the challenge.

Likewise, 5.11s were now routine. As harder and harder climbs went up, they were almost immediately surpassed. Conversations focused only on pushing into the next realm of possibility. Dale Bard, Mark Chapman, Kevin Worrall, George Myers, Billy Westbay, Ray Jardine, Rick Reider, and Bev Johnson joined the chase along with the likes of Jim Erikson, Art Higbee, Henry Barber, and Jim Donini. Close behind was an even bigger rogue's gallery of misfits and mutants, all of them pushing and probing at the next inconceivable first.

"We just fed off each other, and that allowed us to achieve more than if we were on our own," says Billy Westbay. "We were able to discover more of what we could really do...because we could dream big dreams."

No one dreamed bigger than Bridwell. Always stirred to his best performances by competition, Bridwell now set out to set the highest possible standard. Over a two-week period in the summer of 1975 he climbed the Nose in a day (VI 5.10, A2) and put up the Pacific Ocean Wall (VI 5.9, A5)—routes that placed him alone atop the world of technical rock climbing.

"The Nose was great," says Westbay, his partner on both routes. "Our goal was to get back to the Lodge for last call. And when we walked in everybody was so stoked. We couldn't buy a beer."

The P.O. Wall was another matter. "It was really intimidating up [...] And with good rea-

[...]

down, the bird gave in. [...] void below them. "You can take two ropes and go." He didn't, of course, and four days later the team completed the hardest big-wall route on the planet and put high-end Yosemite wall climbing out of the reach of mortals.

"The Pacific Ocean Wall probably changed me more than any other route," Bridwell would say later. "After that, I knew that no matter how bad things looked I could still do it." Quiet, pragmatic, and focused, Bridwell's skill on hard aid has left a lasting impression on everybody who has climbed with him. Nobody has ever mastered great difficulty with less showmanship. "You could never tell where the hard bit was by watching Bridwell," says Westbay. "He just kept at it, never seeming to push it but never seeming to slow down, either. Just really clean and steady."

Now into his mid-thirties and with fifteen years of hard climbing behind him, Bridwell could have walked away after the P.O. Wall and still have been remembered as one of the great rock climbers of his era. Nothing could have been further from his mind. Routes in the mid-to late 1970s like El Cap's Mirage (VI 5.11, A4), Half Dome's Bushido (VI 5.10, A5) and Zenith (VI 5.10, A5), and Mount Watkin's Bob Locke Memorial Buttress (VI 5.11, A4) upped the ante even further.

The Sea of Dreams (VI 5.9, A5), completed in 1978 with Dale Bard and Dave Dingleman, was perhaps the touchstone of the period. This seemingly featureless line linked an intricate network of shallow seams, expanding flakes, and hookable edges. Equipped with multi-RURP belays and including an if-you-fall-you-die pitch, the Sea of Dreams remains a highly respected undertaking and presaged the extreme seriousness of today's hardest aid lines.

Clearly, Bridwell was at the top of his form. No one before or since has owned a place and time in quite the same fashion as he ruled the granite walls of Yosemite National Park. Nobody expected that he was already in the process of transforming himself into one of the world's foremost alpinists.

"I thought you could make money with a slide show of big walls," Bridwell explains, "but the real market seemed to be for alpine climbs. I'd always harbored an alpine desire but California climbers were considered rock jocks. Guys from Colorado and Washington were the ones that went on expeditions."

Recognizing his lack of mountaineering skills, Bridwell had quietly set out to fill the holes in his résumé. He dove in at the deep end. In the summer of 1974 he drove to Canada to attempt the then unclimbed Emperor Face on Mount Robson. Turned back by a recalcitrant car, he instead soloed Washington's Mount Shuksan before returning to the Valley. After the fabulous summer of 1975, he headed for Patagonia.

To anyone else, the unclimbed east face of Cerro Torre might have seemed something of a stretch for a Valley boy who barely knew how to strap on his crampons. In Bridwell's mind, it was the next logical step. The majority of the route was a rock climb and he was the fastest big-wall rock climber on the planet. The ice at the top he would figure out. Unfortunately, his attempt with Kim Carrigan was cut short when the Australian was deported from Bolivia with visa problems. Bridwell didn't get back until the winter of 1979, when he again arrived with the east face of Cerro Torre in mind, but switched his attentions to that tower's Compressor Route after a Christmas Eve encounter with a young American named Steve Brewer. Using borrowed equipment and climbing alpine-style, the two notched the route in just under two days—a shockingly fast time on a route that many believed could only be climbed siege style. Their ascent sent ripples of shock throughout the international climbing community.

Like the P.O. Wall, Cerro Torre also held revelations. Exhausted and pressing their descent into a storm, Bridwell fell from a rappel stance and

" he says of his 150-

"plenty of time passed through the

1-inch webbing around his waist for a harness, the impact Bridwell experienced upon hitting the end of the 9-millimeter haul line snapped his ribs like carrot sticks but saved his life.

It was not to be his last brush with the macabre. Over the next several years each big climb seemed to come equipped with its own unique horrors. A winter ascent of the Moose's Tooth in Alaska with Mugs Stump resulted in a do-or-die rappel from high on the route. He climbed the Shroud on the Grand Jorasse outside Chamonix, France, only to find out that his early mentor Frank Sacherer had been killed by lightning on the same route a year earlier. Returning to Patagonia he dodged storms and falling rock to put up several new routes. He climbed Pumori in winter, traveled to China and Nepal, and nearly died from an intestinal worm contracted during the first coast-to-coast traverse of Borneo with Rick Ridgeway and John Long.

While sponsorships occasionally helped support Bridwell's climbing habit, the majority of his financing came from hard work. In addition to ski patrolling and YOSAR, he toiled on oil rigs, guided, and took whatever odd jobs he could string together. Bridwell's wife, Peggy, whom he had married in 1976, presented the Bird with a son, Layton, in 1979. Bridwell was a proud and doting father. This "magical child" provided new incentive for generating income. Leveraging his climbing skill, Bridwell found work in Hollywood as a rigger and technical advisor, wrote books, and published articles. He also made frequent trips back to the Valley. In the early 1980s he established a string of noteworthy routes including Half Dome's The Big Chill (VI 5.10, A4), Shadows (VI 5.9, A4+) on El Cap, and, one of his all time favorites, Zenyatta Mondatta (VI 5.7, A5), an El Cap horror show that he describes as a mini-Sea of Dreams and "no place for those with a faint heart."

"When I arrived on the scene in the mid-1980s Bridwell was pretty much considered the father of modern aid climbing," confirms Pete Takeda. "Bridwell is in a class alone. A lot of other people have done more routes, but Bridwell was the one who crossed the line. He went after these rotten, expanding features by using heads and hooks and riveting and stuff like that. The things that everybody else was trying to stay away from."

But despite his high profile and sterling résumé, the Bird's stubborn unwillingness to accept limitations gnawed at him. As a second generation of friends drifted away into marriages and careers, he kept at it, constantly searching for new climbs, new partners, new directions.

"We climb onward," Royal Robbins once wrote, reflecting on his ascent of El Cap's North American Wall. "Searching for adventure, searching for ourselves, searching for situations which would call forth our total resources." Climbing has always held those overtones for Bridwell, too. Every summit for him was laced with a sense of incompleteness; every insight braided with a mixture of ambition and alarm; every dream a path stretching out through the graveyards of lost friends and forfeited ambitions.

By the late 1980s Bridwell was beginning to feel the toll of time. Though he was climbing as well as ever, he was a father and for the first time in his life had to scramble for income. He rigged for commercials and a series of made-for-television movies. He did more guiding and became a special trainer for the U.S. Navy Seals. He gave lectures and designed equipment. As always though, he climbed. In 1992, at age fifty, he climbed the Eiger's North Face and was cranking solid 5.12.

I can see Bridwell right now sitting at the table of his modest home in Palm Desert, California. The window open, a cigarette hanging be-

[text obscured] of black coffee in his hand. A steno pad

[text obscured]

Madison, and [text obscured]

died while he was in Patagonia. Guiding in the Tetons, he watched a client fall to his death. The murmur over that one was particularly ugly. Accusations were made; lawsuits filed. The Bird's self-promulgated reputation as a wild man hurt him. "We are," as he has said, "our own creations."

Such self-absorption extracts a price. Bridwell has been called the Chuck Yaeger of serious climbing: someone who was prominent in his time, who gave more than he took, who was peerless as a performer. Americans, however, are prone to taking pleasure in the demise of their idols. "It takes a lot of 'atta boys' to overcome one fuck-up," Bridwell sighs. And the likelihood is that he will be as well remembered for his wild bouts of drinking as for the days and nights he spent chasing the wildest dreams of a generation across the vertical landscape of El Capitan.

No one is more to blame for the misunderstanding than Bridwell. In these days of media intrusiveness and voyeurism he has never made a point of tending very carefully to his image. "Climbing is not that important," he says in his own defense. "It's the camaraderie, it's overcoming elements in myself that matters. The thing that I have enjoyed about it most is that there is no superficiality. The idea is to set a goal and do the best job you can. What are the seven to ten days you spend on a wall compared to life? The values people talk about are imaginary. It's all an illusion. You make yourself up as you go along. You are a viewpoint, a set of beliefs, that's all. People take themselves seriously because they want to be separate. But if you are still conscious when all is said and done, you'll be laughing."

"People trash each other," he sighs. "My gut feeling is that you should judge others the way you judge yourself. I've set high goals for myself and I've always been willing to suffer the consequences if I didn't get there. It's not how good you are, it's your vision, what you contributed. I gave what I had."

⁓

You may be surprised to learn that Jim Bridwell believes in God. He thinks the shit is about to hit the fan. "The world can't go on this way very much longer," he says. "What will happen, I don't know, but it won't be good." He believes that psychedelic drugs were an absolutely positive force in his life, but he doesn't do them anymore. ("They don't make good drugs these days," he complains.)

Bridwell regrets never having had any money. He is sorry that he hasn't spent more time at home. He would very much like to find the funding for another trip to the Himalaya. So it goes.

"To really understand Jim Bridwell," says John Long, "you'd have to go back and climb what he did, when he did it." Both tasks have merit; neither is likely. "I guess," Bridwell replies, "that makes me an enigma."

Not really. Like all of us, Jim Bridwell wants it both ways. He wants people to see him for who he is in the full light of everything he has accomplished. He wants to be respected. He wants to do more big climbs. He wants the past to be seen for what it was and not for the myths and misinformation that cloy at him. He wants to be half as much appreciated in his own country as he has been abroad. He wants most to be remembered for the good he has done, and that might be an impossible request from someone who has lived his life like a climb—minimal gear, maximum commitment—throwing everything he had at every moment. "Americans are tough on their heroes," says John Long. "The things that made him so good as a climber make him a pretty easy target for people who don't really know him. I know it bothers him, but his answer has always been to go put up another route. To let his climbing speak for him."

PART IV
Humor

BAH

I know not what it be, but I go to it laughing...
—Starbuck, *Moby Dick*

$\backsim$

He awoke so suddenly he gasped at the sensation of finding himself upright. For an instant his hands still held the image of rock and snow and his legs were spread to receive the impact of his fall, but his feet stirred only dirt and his arms embraced nothing but his dreams. He wrestled momentarily with the shape of reality and found it worse. The dust and stench of the hut gagged him and he wheezed pathetically on the bronchial fluid awash in his lungs. The throb from his ankle was excruciating. He fell back heavily on his air mattress, beads of sweat running down his cheeks and eyes bloodshot with pain. Never in his life had Linus Gregg felt more terrified or alone.

He woke up again just at dawn. Outside the thick mud and dung walls he could hear the village coming to life: the rustle of sheep being driven to the meadows, the hooves clicking on the path stones to the arrhythmic harmonies of infantile Balti herdsmen. Unable to sleep any longer, Linus eased himself into a sitting position. He heated a bowl of water on his small Primus stove and drank a pot of weak tea. As the first bright bolts of sunrise reached the hut he gently shifted his feet to the warm rectangle of light that illuminated the center of the room.

His head ached miserably. The acrid, urine-and-smoke odor of the air seemed to finger every pore of his skin. He yawned and thought, and as he thought his chest sank and his shoulders curved down toward his knees. The fall. He felt condemned to relive the accident through every gap in concentration the rest of his life. And always, when he thought about it—an ignominiously spastic stumble on some loose talus—the idiocy of it, the damnable *injustice* of it seemed to nag at him as much as the injury itself. He had sent the others on and a detail of porters had carried him away from the wreckage of his Himalayan climbing career down to Askole where he had found a hut on the edge of the village. Here he would await the expedition's return. The pain of the broken

preceding lunch. On this particular morning, however, he had been asleep for perhaps no more than half an hour when it occurred to him that he was being watched. At first the realization had little impact on him. His western idiosyncrasies had frequently attracted spectators since his arrival in Askole. But this time when he rolled over and turned toward the door there was no rapid shuffling of feet, no whispering and laughter. Instead, he met a gaze of steady, utterly open curiosity. On a face, he later wrote in his journal, kinder and more honest than any he had ever seen.

She was not beautiful. She didn't look much different than any of the other females in the village he had glimpsed darting past his door. Yet, she possessed him. Resting his head on the pillow of his arms, Linus took advantage of the shadows to study her carefully. She was lithe and small. Her knotted, black hair glimmered in the sunlight with its sheen of red dust. The smell of her filled the room. His heart leapt at her unintentional sexuality and ran a heat through his dreams that left him nervously praying for her return the following day.

When she came back everything in his life changed. She became the point of his sufferance. He sat dumb as a potato through her third and fourth visitations. On the fifth day, though, he was ready. He sat cross-legged in the center of the room, his face and bandaged leg bathed in a shaft of dusted sunlight. As she approached the door he smiled, bowing slightly and stretched out his long arm, his hand up and open, motioning her into the room. She followed his gesture and then looked back to his eyes. Linus grinned and nodded. His face flushed. His heart beat against the inside of his chest so loudly he was sure she must hear it. His legs trembled. She turned to inspect the room, entered, and sat opposite him against the far wall. She stayed for an hour and then left.

They repeated the tableau each morning for a week. She never stayed longer and they never spoke. The physical distance between them never changed. Their eyes and expressions shared the exquisite pain of atavistic propriety and refused longing. The room was hushed by the subtle mime of their mutual wanting.

For his part, Linus felt an intelligence and clarity that he had never before experienced in anything but climbing. Yet, after twenty days of meeting, a morning came when she did not return. Nor did she the next day. Although Linus had thought himself emotionally prepared for this eventuality, he was not. He limped down to the river and threw pebbles into the whirlpools and eddies. He had no appetite for dinner. He went to bed early, slept fitfully, and arose before dawn. She was standing quietly at the door. She came slowly toward Linus and huddled in the fold of his arms as if she had all her life. In the instant before they fell back among the sighs of down and shadows, the room seemed to fill with white light.

His parents were devastated. He tried to make things sound right, but as he spoke his mother and father cast furtive, perplexed glances at one another, and when he had finished, he realized the plausibility of his story must have seemed as remote to them as Rawalapindi. There was no tranquillity in the stillness that came. Sprinklers on the front lawn clicked and whispered and the sun slowly dropped to flash acute planks of brilliant orange light across the white walls of the living room. Beside the front door a plasticene doe stood in its frozen graze among the dwarf rhododendrons and junipers. The rich aroma of his homecoming dinner was drawn outside through the air conditioning and into the lugubrious southern California heat which waited for evening to settle its weight in the asphalt pores of the driveway. The silence remained.

Linus tried to be philosophical about his parents' despair. He did not enjoy it, although he accepted it as he had his initial isolation in the village. He was in love and naive enough to believe that once they saw and met Bah, once they understood the sincerity and depth of his feel-

nim, could she possibly

had they ever done, they wanted to know, that he should want to hurt them like this? His father begged him to be realistic. Mrs. Gregg sat erect among the pastel cushions of their huge, white couch, her handkerchief rising to touch barely controlled tears.

In the months that followed Linus busied himself visiting the Pakistani consulate in Los Angeles. He went two or three times a week and spent hours filling out visa applications. He hired a lawyer to help him with the paperwork and found an Urdu/English phrasebook, which he studied conscientiously. He tried to talk about other things at the dinner table, but as the day of Bah's arrival came closer it was hard for him to contain his exuberance.

Against the advice of both her husband and her family physician, Mrs. Gregg decided to go to the airport to meet Bah. Compelled by some ageless maternal instinct to share in the tragedies of her son's life as she had in its glories, Mrs. Gregg walked stiffly through the long corridors of the airport, her husband holding her by one elbow. When the ramp dropped into place and her son dashed forward, and the source of all her worry and concern stepped at last into the California sunlight, Linus' mother quietly lifted a feathery hand to one cheek and collapsed. She was silent as the paramedics lifted her onto a stretcher, but Mr. Gregg turned to his only child with a glare of such choleric intensity that his expression was more eloquent than any words his outrage might have found.

Linus made no effort to explain to Bah why he was not taking her home. He simply got on the freeway and turned north. Her eyes, their only means of communication, seemed to accept this passively, without panic or misinterpretation. For a long time they went without making a sound. Linus drove too fast, gripping the steering wheel with both hands. Bah slipped down on the seat and lay with her head in his lap. She did not lift her eyes to the miracle of Orange County or the violent lights of L.A. East of the city Linus turned toward the desert and they both seemed to relax. They spent their first night together in nearly six months at a trailer court outside Bakersfield with the dry wind undulating the cottonwoods and wrapping them both in memories.

In the morning Linus was more cheerful. They continued north. Bah watched now in mesmerized fascination as the verdant bowl of the San Joaquin Valley replaced the dry grit of the desert. Linus told her they were headed for Yosemite. May, he said, was the perfect time to be there. She blinked her eyes and sat facing him attentively. While she may not have understood a word he said, she knew clearly the tone of his contentment. Linus turned on the radio and clapped his thigh with his hand. Everything will be cool there, he told her. He brushed the side of her face with one hand and smiled. No one will even notice us there, he said. The only people there in the spring are Japanese tourists and rock climbers. He laughed about that and his features grew flushed and animate. He called the climbers the last moral society left on earth and told her about the white granite towers, the yellow glow of lanterns in Camp 4, and the clink of hardware. He made Yosemite sound as if it were the Paris of the 1980s: full of expatriate geniuses, bright and eclectic and crazy as the moon.

Perhaps he even believed it himself. But when they arrived and set up their tent, Linus discovered that he had once again underestimated the hard tissue of the human heart. Even among his closest friends there was laughter. He couldn't tell whether Bah noticed it or not, but he could hear it at night around nearby campfires and he heard it in the murmuring gossip that followed them wherever they went like the babble of stones in a brook. People pointed. The rudest of the tourists took photographs, and teenagers shouted things from cars.

Still, Linus did not give up on Yosemite. Partially because he was being stubborn, but more because he could think of no place else to go.

broken wooden ties nailed to the polished shield of granite, Bah kept pace easily with Linus. In the early evening they stood side by side overlooking the shaded Valley below them. It was the best day of their lives together.

They tried a similar hike up to Yosemite Falls but they met other tourists: gawkers and pointers chortling behind bends in the trail. They found another route down, but by then it didn't matter. Sometimes nothing does. Linus had been so dwarfed by love that for months nothing else in his life had mattered. The world had been miniaturized by the enormity of his affection. He had martyred himself for an ideal which, now that he lived it, he found he no longer quite trusted. As first-time lovers so often are, he was ruined by his doubts. He wanted the proof of love, the words more than the essence of it. He ignored rather than sought the symptoms of his anger. He began to mistrust her silence. He challenged her commitment to him, although he knew Bah had abandoned everything she knew in the world to be with him. He sought the most facile signs of conjugality and denied every indication that he saw them. He lost faith in himself and felt deceived, and in his self-pity he created the end of everything he wanted.

They quit Yosemite and drove east again, the two of them stinging with emptiness. Like all *sennins*—mountain lunatics—Linus sought wisdom and refuge once more in solitude, so they drove into the desert of the High Sierra and waited. His moods came like the weather: sometimes petulant and hot, other times cold and stormy; impossible to predict one day to the next. They shared their set of gestures and nothing more. They did not eat or sleep together. They never touched or spoke. Their eyes never met. They only waited.

Linus withered in the heat. There was a little money left in the car. He could have driven into Bishop easily enough for supplies, but that would have meant more laughter or leaving Bah and he could bring himself to face neither alternative. He could not go home. There was no food and water and there were no answers. So he meditated and starved and waited, hatless and burning his own angry fire in the noonday sun. Bah stood her distance and did not interrupt. A hundred generations of ancestral experience told her not to. It was her role to wait. She had no other notion of what to do. She reached back along the shallow plane of their relationship for some solution and found nothing but shattered images of the past without a clue to the future.

On the seventh day of their retreat Bah strayed off and explored their surroundings. The terrain was comforting in its similarity to the Karakorum gorge where she was born. The air was sweet with the delicate scent of wildflowers and sage. In a depression beneath some boulders she found a pool of stagnant, brackish water. She drank deeply from it and rested in the shade. When she felt stronger she trotted quickly back to the campsite, but when she arrived she found Linus lying on the ground unconscious.

She came near him carefully. She nuzzled against him as she had so often in the past...and in the same white heat that had once filled the hut she understood that Linus would sweep open no more rooms for her. She backed away slowly and for a long time simply stood and watched him.

When it grew cooler in the early evening she returned to the waterhole to drink. As she made her way back to camp, she stopped to graze on several small patches of grass and managed to paw some bits of food out of the dirt near the open door of the car. The nylon sides of the tent luffed in the soft mountain breezes while sun-smudged magenta clouds gathered in mounds along the horizon.

She turned her back on the sunset to look out east over the great, darkling sprawl of Nevada and saw America for the first time through her own eyes. She saw pin-point lights from distant ranches and the inky spread of meadows and grass. Bleating quietly she started down,

POONTANGA

My job is out there with the fundamental forces.

—Michael Moschen

⌐

NOTE: *The Humboltkin Letters, of which this journal is comprised, are viewed by many knowledgeable observers as a major discovery, not only in terms of what they represent as a documentation of great adventure, but for what they have added to the store of twentieth-century literature. Many consider the collection to be an instant classic. As in all great works of nonfiction, this material provides us with insights on both a remarkable event and an astonishing character. The event: the much debated first consummation of Poontanga by a Himalyan expedition; the character: none other than that great adventurer and diarist, David Humboltkin.*

In editing these pages for publication, extensive research has been carried out so as to leave no doubt in anyone's mind as to the authenticity of the journal. Both the penmanship and style of the original manuscript have been identified by friends and members of the late climber's family as his own. Additional corroboration was provided by Dr. Humboltkin's roommates during his freshman year at the University of Colorado, where it is theorized he first became seriously engaged in the search for Poontanga. Dr. Humboltkin would have undoubtedly been flattered by growing interest in Poontanga exhibited by so many modern expeditions. As is implied time and again throughout the following pages, Dr. Humboltkin went to the mountains not just for Poontanga, but to show others the way.

Here is the journal then, with no further comment other than to simply ask that you attempt to understand the enormity of the undertaking before you judge the author for his all too human weaknesses.

1 September 1959, The Khomanghettit Glacier

I have dreamed during most of my adult life of someday standing in this exact spot. In truth, I have seen myself standing here since before I even knew such a place existed beyond a boy's wildest caprice. Yet since

1956, when the expedition began to take the shape of destiny, I have made this adventure—this mountain—my life. In other moments I have composed a thousand pages of prose to describe the sights and feelings I imagined I would experience upon first viewing the incredible beauty

ply. To the south the vast, mile-thick, gray carpet of the monsoon covers the entire mass of the Indian subcontinent. To my right and to my left and always above me are the mountains! They are impossibly beautiful. Frightening and at the same time alluring. Impassive and yet sensual beyond resisting. And there in their midst spreading out ridges toward us as if welcoming the challenge: Poontanga!

The traditional approach of expeditions to Poontanga has proven to be as theoretically sound and realistically ineffective as traditional answers usually are. No doubt it is the sensible route, the ultimately rational line; it assumes the obvious and exploits the apparent weaknesses of the mountain. But it will not go. Sir Anthony Twillingbyrd-Smythe's ill-starred British attempt decided that conclusively. While they were able to easily overcome the initial problems of Poontanga's twin guardian peaks to the north, Hoon-kee and Do-ree, the expedition floundered and was eventually turned back by the incredible complexities involved in traversing the Plain of Snows. Poontanga, it seems, does not reward subtlety with conquest; she awaits boldness and commitment! Thus will we be taking a more technically demanding line, ascending the western leg called "Idareya" by the natives. A bold thrust along this inside line, if executed with calm, courage, and timing should deliver us our goal. We do not, of course expect it to come easily.

Our team, as has already been well publicized, is an international one. Besides me, we are two Serbians, an Afghan, a Morrocan dissident, an unemployed fortune-teller named Friggo, whose place of origin is unknown, a Viennese, and our three faithful Sherpas—Houi, Doui, and Loui. Much has been made of the fact that no international expedition has ever successfully climbed a major Himalayan peak. Failure in almost every case has been attributed to problems of leadership and accepting responsibility. We feel we have prepared for this and will hopefully overcome it by assembling a team entirely lacking any sense of responsibility or interest in leading anything.

But enough about us. Tomorrow before dawn we begin climbing! I will diligently try to maintain this journal to the best of my ability, until we have either reached the top or suffered whatever else chance has in store for us.

7 September 1959, Camp II—Ghettin Klosar Glacier

Camp II has been established and we are in the process of investigating sites for advance camps along the ridge. Apart from the daily drudgery of trekking down to Camp I and then back up, life here takes on a routine of its own. One has to prod himself to acknowledge the staggeringly beautiful scenery surrounding us. We settle into our own formulas. As I write, Lkjhgfdski—one of the Serbians—seems content to be constantly scrubbing out his underwear. Lobisa, a prince in his native Afghanistan, toys with his pet weapons. Our Sherpas, on the other hand, seem quite content to spend their spare time sitting in a small circle passing around a pipe filled with some loathsome-smelling native tobacco which, despite its bizarre stench, only seems to enhance their remarkable cheerfulness!

As the critical moments of the climb seem to be yet in front of us, now seems an appropriate time to take a moment and deal with some of the criticism that has so long surrounded our choice of Dr. Armando Flies as team physician. As you will doubtless recall, there was open skepticism in some quarters as to whether his specialty in large animal vasectomy was adequate to our needs. I will not honor that kind of thinking by calling it controversial. Since having joined us in Calcutta, Armo (as he is affectionately referred to) has endeared himself to all of us. His performance in the field of medicine has been thoroughly professional and, at times, even superhuman. I hope it will put to rest all doubts of his

alive by a fraternity boy in black boxer shorts. How clearly I recall the doctor placing a comforting hand on my knee and explaining that dreams are simply a sign that the beings who control us on the planet Xephrone are happy and that my inner child was receiving nothing more than a gentle cosmic spanking. One that he would be glad to duplicate.

As with all Himalayan expeditions, the effects of altitude constitute the great unknown for us. Yet Dr. Flies' daily examinations of climbers returning from the high camps have so far prevented anyone from developing either hair on their palms or the desire to run for high elective office. I lay much of his success to the crystalline powder he discovered while shopping for medication in Kathmandu. Inhaled through either nostril on a regular basis, this medication not only eliminates the headaches and colds so frequent above 17,000 feet, but has also had a most salubrious effect on our morale! Personally, it has stabilized my blood pressure, spared me the discomfort of having to eat, and allowed me to read the entire English edition of Thomas Mann's *Magic Mountain* in just under 8.5 minutes. A record, I believe, at this altitude.

Tomorrow we will be moving into the monolithic blue ice folds of the upper Odsyen Glacier. At this time of year the seracs overhang one another like huge vaults, building and growing sodden with wet snow until finally they collapse. I would be less than realistic to believe that the possibility of death was not concealed therein and less than fair if I were to risk a premature ending to these pages without first thanking some of those who made the expedition fact. While it was our desire to draw financial support from as many sources as possible and thereby remain a "people's expedition," special thanks are still called for. We were, of course, particularly gratified by Senator Kennedy's interest in our project and for his words of encouragement. Likewise, we are grateful to Sid and Erma Goldman, owners of the Broadway Deli, for their contribution of a life-sized swan made entirely from raw chicken livers; to the manufacturer's of Stephenson tents (to whom we will be sending all photography); the citizens of Intercourse, Pennsylvania; and, of course, Dr. Freud without whom we would simply have been climbing.

17 September 1959, Camp II

Snow squalls these past ten days have made any movement impossible. I am pleased to note that my relationship with the darkies has been superb. They have been both docile and helpful throughout, treating us with the necessary blend of hospitality and deference that has made them so highly thought of. As a whole, they are open, unsophisticated, and charming. They respond to strength with strength, and if the summit falls to us, the burden of credit belongs to them. Indeed, the memory of this expedition which will outlast all others is that of our last night in the Sherpa hamlet of Mastacahd. There, totally to our surprise, we were invited to take part in a ceremony of parting and farewell as old as their culture itself. In this dance we were given a handful of wooden trinkets in exchange for our American Express travelers checks. (I rather hate to say it, but I believe the poor fools were fascinated by the colors!)

Later, sitting in the home of our *sidbar* watching television, his father confessed to me that as soon as his youngest son returned from Oxford he was thinking about moving to the Middle East where he had heard the climate was kinder and that money was to be made in oil. Sadly, there was no explaining to him the genetic inability of the Arab to fully exploit this natural resource.

19 September 1959, Camp II

Snow continues to fall, though the sun broke through for a short time today and portends better weather on the morrow. Lkjhgfdski and I will leave at dawn and attempt to establish Camp III. Morale remains

21 September 1959, Camp III

Camp III having been quickly established in a huge snow cavern beneath an outward jutting mass of rock, we are about to begin the climb toward the knoll on the edge of the plateau called the Knee. We are carrying enough equipment to place Camp IV should luck be with us. Its projected altitude would be just over 23,000 feet, higher than any of us have ever been before. Thanks to Dr. Flies, we seem to be acclimatizing well, though life at 21,800 feet above sea level has certainly proved to have its own oddities. The feeling of lethargy is constant. At times merely getting out of one's sleeping sack becomes an unimaginably difficult task. It is so easy to allow oneself the continuing pleasure of sleep. The fact that Myerbeck and Friggo arrived in camp today has greatly improved our morale. Even Lkjhgfdski, who has stayed in his tent talking to his teddy bear for the last few days was laughing in no time over their hysterical antics. They really are awfully jolly fellows! Only this morning we found them outside their tent, stark naked, holding hands, laughing like fools, dancing the Tarantella and swatting each other with wet gym towels! I was lucky enough to snap several photos of this which I shall forward along with my article to *National Geographic.*

28 September 1959, Camp IV

After an epic seven-day struggle we have finalized Camp IV. The weather seems to be changing again for the worse. We thought we had been overtaken by the tempest last night. Fortunately, the howling and whining proved to be nothing more than Friggo suffering from having eaten a local specialty prepared with yak dung and small pebbles.

2 October 1959, Camp V

Tragedy has marred the conclusion of our first month on the mountain. Lobisa, accompanied by the three Sherpas, set out yesterday to find a location for Camp VI. They had negotiated most of the major difficulties when they were overtaken by a storm. For eight hours they continued climbing, struggling like men possessed, determined to either succeed in establishing a sixth camp or perish in the effort. At 7:30 P.M., in near-complete darkness, with the storm swirling around them, they struggled over the lip of a small platform beside an ice gully and elected to bivouac there. Unfortunately, the platform was already the site of Camp IV which they had somehow circumnavigated in the maelstrom. This misfortune was further compounded when it was discovered in the morning that in seeking to find a solid anchor for their guy-line, one of the Sherpas had driven a snow stake through Lkjhgfdski, who was squatting in the snow relieving himself.

Quite naturally we have all been greatly saddened by this event. All day long a debate has raged back and forth as to whether using his body as a natural anchor corrupts the validity of our route. I plan to write an immediate appeal to the British Mountaineering Council who I anticipate will reply sometime prior to the millennium.

12 October 1959, Camp V

We have completed our chain of high camps along the entire length of the Idareya Leg of Poontanga. From the entrance of my tent I can look up and see the smooth, distinctly shaped summit. As drawn and soul-spent as the higher camps make one feel, the nearness of our goal still stirs the heart. Victory finds its way into letters and images. Tomorrow, provided the weather holds, four of us will try to turn those words and dreams into reality.

At a moment like this the mind automatically wanders back to other attempts. To the northeast I can clearly make out the route of the British

ness is not, of itself, enough. My years in America, however, have left me more convinced than ever that success with Poontanga demands an entirely unique style of integrated expeditioning. Certainly, wisdom, patience and sensitivity are vital—even if only temporarily so. Persistence is probably equally important. Indeed, so successful have these attributes been for us that I feel almost assured this approach will be put to use by tomorrow's young people!

No matter. Friggo and Myerbeck have pushed on to establish Camp VI! The additional loads required to support a summit push will be ferried up this afternoon. If all goes well and according to plan, the summit could be ours by the fifteenth!

22 October 1959, Camp VI

It has snowed almost continuously since our arrival at Camp VI ten days ago. Movement of any kind is impossible. We have rationed our food to the point that hunger nags incessantly, making any semblance of sleep impossible. Dozing and awakening seem to run into one state of supreme lethargy. There is little or no talk, only the constant groans. The clouds keep us in perpetual night. We have been urinating into our cups to avoid the unbearable cold outside. We cling together like spoons to avoid losing heat. Strangely, I have the strongest desire to eat raw oysters...

26 October 1959, Camp VI

Now Madness!!

Friggo and Myerbeck deserted camp today during a short respite in the storm. We begged them not to. We warned them, cajoled them, reasoned with them, threatened them physically, and even went so far as to offer them engraved belly-button rings if they would only stay. All to no avail. Myerbeck said he was "just going to run down and order a Quarter Pounder with Cheese, an order of fries, a Coke, and change back from his dollar." Friggo, whose teeth were still buried in Myerbeck's thigh, said nothing. The poor, brave fools! The storm engulfed them before they even reached the ropes. Beyond all doubt they are lost. Since then Lobisa and I have withdrawn into our private misery. Occasionally our eyes will meet, then dart to some safe corner of the tent where there is no danger of contact. I have been watching him all afternoon and have concluded that he is clearly insane. As I write this he is nibbling at his boots, which I am certain he thinks is very clever, but which I personally find repugnant. We shall see what immigration has to say about such behavior.

27 October 1959, Camp VI

Awoke this morning to a perfectly clear, windless day. It brought with it some good news and some bad news. The good news is that Loui, the Sherpa leader, was able to struggle his way through chest-deep snow to bring us a supply of much-needed food. The bad news is that Lobisa, who was in no state to deal with such an emotional overload, cracked like a china cup and ate the entire contents of Loui's pack. This has left him in no condition to climb. I will send him down as soon as he is fit lest he devour the tent in my absence. The final push for Poontanga I shall make myself.

28 October 1959, Camp VI

The weather is again clear. I have sent Lobisa down. The time has come to climb. I feel serene and am happy to be alone yet strangely unable to organize my thoughts. Perhaps the animal sense of having come to a point of no return makes me place too much weight on going ahead. In any case, I will carry this journal with me to the summit. In the event that I am unable to return it will remain there as a testament to my

Unfortunately, David Humboltkin was able to make only one more entry in his journal. The handwriting would seem to indicate that his fingers may have been frozen at the time. It is theorized that Humboltkin completed his attempt on Poontanga shortly after nightfall. Realizing that it was futile to descend in the dark, he instead chose to stay where he was. His mental state had, in all likelihood, degenerated by this time to the point where he was no longer able to reason effectively, thus accounting for this last, terse entry: " I, David Humboltkin, do hereby forfeit all my insurance benefits and earthly wealth, should I survive, to rub MM with raw garlic. "

All these many years later it is hard to place his triumph in its proper historical perspective. Humboltkin was thirty-seven years old and the sole member of his expedition to reach Poontanga. Nowadays, it is not unusual for several members of a single expedition to do the same thing. Sadly, with Poontanga being so much more achievable these days, it is no longer possible to experience what that great mountaineer-explorer must have felt upon finally realizing his lifelong ambition. Poontanga was, at long last, his! As we must admire his courage and daring, so too must we envy him that moment of exultation that few of us are ever privileged to repeat.

CANNON MOUNTAIN BREAKDOWN

Every time the established order of things collapses, security is destroyed and everything that was protected by law, be it man-made or natural, is exposed to ferociousness and unreasoning brutality.

—Guy de Maupassant

NOTE: *Shortly after 1 P.M. on Sunday, August 12, 1973, Mark Lawrence and Dana Jones fell to their deaths from the eighth pitch of Sam's Swan Song on Cannon Mountain. As they fell, the rope connecting them caught on an overhang 250 feet above the ground and near the center of the face. Their bodies hung there most of the day while a recovery team was organized. Responding to news of the accident while on the radio, a crowd of local residents and tourists gathered on the highway below to watch. To watch what is unknown. The following day a Boston newspaper published a full front-page photograph of the two dead climbers suspended from the face. Sales were excellent.*

A Tenuous Ride

It is August and a Sunday, the middle of a long vacation and the end of the summer. Charlie Pride turns slowly on a silver cassette. Two and a half hours of the same song sung in a bass nasal about bad women and shooting stars, long-haul rigs, dead-end roads, and the just-plain-folks-heartache down-and-out-drag-ass blues. Behind the wheel of the Jeep Big Al sings along when the words come to mind or when he isn't drinking Sunsweet prune juice out of a half-empty black bottle. It's hot—85, maybe 90 degrees already—and the sweat rolls down his arms and off his eyebrows, but he leaves the windows rolled up so he can hear every note of the music, every magical phrase. Beside him on the front seat, crumpled in the heat like an old newspaper, dressed in a greasy trench coat stolen out of some forgotten basement bar in Saratoga Falls and giving off the sweet stench of a two-week bender, L, the People's Choice, drops his head back against the door and groans. He's waking up not feeling well for the seventh day in a row. This constant cycle of drunkenness and suffering has not done him any good: His mouth is open

with rotting, week-old bologna sandwiches and sour dill pickles, rear-end padded from the floor by a mildewing stack of *Car & Driver* magazines, I—your author—am beginning to stir into consciousness. For the first time in several days there is good news in awakening. My teeth have begun to feel hard again. The blood has stopped oozing between the sutures over my right eye and formed a neat Wisconsin-shaped scab. There is no immediately noticeable discomfort anywhere but in my eyes. Since falling asleep while wearing my contact lenses several days ago everything has appeared in soft focus and sort of sepia-toned, like watching an old movie. By now I am beginning to adjust to the way certain objects seem to glow: things like the back of Big Al's head, a bottle of bourbon lying on its side on the floor, shreds of a Playboy foldout strewn among the down and nylon, and, of course, the early-morning face of Cannon Mountain just now rising over green foothills 15 miles in front of us.

"Now thet's soome fookin' picture, in't it?" Big Al asks, canting his head towards the mountain and turning off the tape recorder. L belches and rolls forward onto the floor, crushing beer cans with his head and hips. Big Al answers for himself without seeming to notice. "Yeah, you people goot the bloody scenery all right," he says, "you joost doona knew enough ta be leavin' it bloody weel aloone."

The way he's talking has me flashing back to a week earlier and the vision of Big Al holding an empty gin bottle by the neck and saying similar things about the Shawanagunks. Calling them a great American tragedy. Saying it couldn't happen anywhere else and God knows certainly not in his own sainted native Scotland. "Imagine any mon standin' still fer havin' ta pay ta climb whoot the Good Lard hae poot there fer him ta climb fer free!" He'd harangued the crowd at the Überfall at the top of his lungs like that for half an hour, flailing at the air with his hands to draw them into his outrage and pounding the asphalt with his forehead from time to time to get their attention. "No!" he'd told them, "revolution is thee oonly way o' savin' these moontains! Ra-vo-lu-tion!" On and on. It was a rambling, drunken, and fearful diatribe, and several hours later L, sitting beside me with his face in a house salad, wept with residual emotion at the mere telling of the story, tears mixing on his cheeks with red-orange smears of Thousand Island dressing. But the rest of the clientele in the Howard Johnson's restaurant had turned away and just looked embarrassed.

As the reminiscence fades, I move to shift positions, and somewhere in the morass of dirty clothes, half-eaten sandwiches, and flattened Tuborg cans beneath me my hand falls upon a book. The tone of the last three weeks has not led me to expect, say, a volume of Euclid hidden in some dark corner of the Jeep, but curiosity has hold of me and I reach for it. It's the Shawanagunks guidebook. New from Paragon's Sporting Goods only a few weeks ago, it is now wet and pasty with a semicongealed combination of mud and beer and piss and vomit and God knows what else. There is a small .22-caliber-sized hole in the back from a demonstration given in a New Paltz tavern on bolt placement. Whole sections have been torn out and lost or used for toilet paper and discarded. I let it slip from my hands and fall back to the floor where it splats like a kitchen sponge.

Up front Big Al is turning the Jeep around a broad curve where we momentarily lose sight of Cannon as it sinks behind the skeletal framework of a new overpass extending I-89 into the bowels of the national forest. Halfway through the cloverleaf the road straightens into a seedy line of neon signs, abandoned shacks, shoulder-to-shoulder motels, steak houses, gas stations, antique shops, restaurants, trailer parks, pools, hot-dog stands, real estate offices, and billboards. The face, when it reappears, is crisscrossed by a maze of high-tension electrical wire.

the driver's seat and goes to the back of the jeep, steps aside to let me fall past and then begins digging through the duffel bag.

"Thoought I'd take a phooto er two, you know," he grins. "Might as weel be gettin' out an' stretchin' yer legs. It ain't far new."

I stand and watch a light appear dimly in L's open eye. Almost unconsciously he begins making the moves to open the door, doing what he is aware in some corridor of his mind he has been told to do. Son of an iron-willed immigrant Russian meat cutter and his even more iron-willed ball cutter of a wife, now a junior partner in some faceless Wall Street law firm with an office on the eighty-fifth floor of the World Trade Center, his own personal secretary, thank you, and a boss who hates him, L has mastered the art of achieving success through creative obeisance. According to the doctrine of L this craft consists entirely of nodding one's head enthusiastically while repeating the last four words spoken by anyone in authority and phrasing them as a question. Though the woman with whom he most often associates is a success-driven Scientologist, L gets by on Ginsberg and guilelessness. In a jungle where quick wits and a ninja spirit are the tools of prosperity, L earns six figures a year unarmed. The front door swings open and the People's Choice drops his legs over the edge of the seat.

"Get the guidebook, will you?" he whispers in my direction, "I gotta do another drop."

Confrontation

In front of the Jeep, framed by the growing cluster of cars, trucks, tour buses, station wagons, and trailers queuing across the street trying to get into Fantasy Forest at Natureland, Big Al is chortling contentedly to himself and spreading the legs of his tripod. In his free hand he is holding a brand new, jet-black, $740 Nikon Photomic FTN with a 200-millimeter, high-diffusion zoom lens and adjust-o-matic f-stop setter. There has been a controversy surrounding this camera: The details involving Big Al's having come up with enough money to buy it are shrouded with innuendo and talk of a suitcase carried empty to Marrakech and returned to Great Britain weighing nearly twelve pounds. From my experience the story lacks the subtlety that typifies Big Al's best work, but at worst it is no worse than the angel food cake I saw him squash into the face of the woman who started the fight in the bar in New Paltz. I was standing right behind him then, too, and marveling at his moves.

Anyway, he's got the camera up on his tripod now and is turning heads like crazy. Which, next to beer farts and flipping occupied out-houses, Big Al likes better than just about anything else a man can do in the vertical plane. He's in the process of running off the first couple of frames when the motor court manager comes running toward him.

He is wearing a sweat-stained jacket and, beneath that, a white shirt coming untucked from his alligator belt. Tranquilizers rattle in his pocket and his face is aglow with that great old American territorial imperative. In general, there is a ferociousness about him that one can just tell is not going to take kindly to a trio of shirtless thirty-year-old hippies standing around in the front yard. The People's Choice staggers toward him, meeting him 20 feet in front of the Jeep.

"Excuse me, sir," L mutters, holding out his ball of pages torn from the Shawanagunks guidebook, "Do you know where can a guy take a dump around here?" The manager does not respond at first. He is taken back a little by L's appearance, uncertain whether the People's Choice is actually retarded or merely being unpleasant.

"Drop dead," he finally sneers, and then watches with open-mouthed horror as L, looking for all the world like a Times Square pervert, stumbles to a tree, leans back against it, and lowers his trousers. For an instant the manager is frozen in place, his eyes growing to the size of Ping-

Big Al looks over his shoulder at the manager, back to adjusting the focus ring on his lens. On the road, tourists coming out of the Dairy Queen and heading south in their Winnebagos or pitching Crackerjacks at Clark's Trained Bears slow down to stare. In a state like New Hampshire, where the license plates read "Live Free or Die" and the governor thinks the John Birch Society is a left-wing plot, when a property owner yells "police" at out-of-state hippies, the outcome is almost certain to be entertaining.

"Hey," the manager growls after a moment, "what's the matter, you don't hear so good or something?" He shoves the end of the brand new lens, swinging the camera around and nearly toppling it.

Big Al stands.

"All right, luv," Big Al says, low-down and most intimately, "you want ta play games, do you? Now I'm goin' ta bite yer fookin' noose oof."

Actually, the "want ta play games" business doesn't mean much. Showy, but harmless. Big Al's way of dealing with almost any unpleasant situation. I have overheard him say worse to pinball machines, bartenders, usherettes, cigarette vendors, postage stamps, oval carabiners, and even his own beloved Grandma'ma during a trans-Atlantic telephone call. It is the word "luv" that concerns me. It is too personal, too extravagant and out of character not to hold some ominous connotation. Apparently the manager has the same second sense, as he immediately backs off a step or two and rapidly begins to talk down the whole "unfortunate misunderstanding" until, sensing an avenue of escape, he pivots on one heel and sprints in the direction of the motel. Unfortunately, he collides almost instantly with L, who is still squatting beside the tree. They both topple over, the manager sliding through L's mess like a beached pickerel, squealing at the top of his lungs and coming back to his feet with pages of the Shawanagunks guidebook stuck to his side and arms. Big Al immediately swivels his camera around and snaps a picture of him.

The People's Choice gets up slowly, tugging at his pants and shaking his head. Big Al takes up his tripod with one hand, L with the other and comes back to the Jeep. He tosses in the People's Choice, hands me his camera, and slips behind the wheel.

"Bad day," he is mumbling to himself as the Jeep spins back onto the road, spraying a Greyhound charter bus with gravel, "I kin joost fookin' feel it."

Camping Out

The Lafayette Campground is lousy with its usual August squalor of humanity when we arrive, the price nobody ever gets used to paying for the convenience of a National Park within a day's drive of thirty million people. Big Al miraculously finds, and then squeezes the Jeep into, the parking place left between a rusted Datsun coupe and a miniature white camper top mounted like a sheep on the back of a red Ford pickup. The owner of the truck and his wife are sitting out on the grass in aluminum lawn chairs with a barbecue and an ice chest full of beer. They are watching a battery-powered television. The man is wearing a baseball cap, flip-down sunglasses, a Budweiser T-shirt, madras shorts, black socks, and sandals. Beneath the sun reflector his wife is holding up to her face she is wrapped, as if by bailing wire, in Day-Glo short-shorts and a tie-dye halter without which she would spread out formlessly as an amoebae and probably ooze off her chair. Monty Hall has her laughing hard enough to shake loose a few curlers from her hair. Big Al takes her picture, too.

The routine we have established for lunch leads me to take some canned meat, a bottle of Beefeater's gin, and a couple of six-packs out of the car. We sit down with it under a small tree. The People's Choice comes around a little after he has had something to drink. He is still

sprinkle his Spam; Kodaks, Kleenex, Polaroid,

radios, hot dogs, hamburgers, french fries, melted ice cream cones, and the endless crowds of pale and misshapen city bodies, screaming children, and snarling suburban pets. Across the road a line has formed near the access to the Falling Waters Trail up Mount Lafayette. Most of the hikers are young, long-haired, and carrying huge packs jammed full of sparkling new camping gear. Interspersed among them are a few family groups: overweight parents dressed in golf clothes and carrying Thermos tanks that click with ice, puffing along behind their petulant twelve-year-olds. No one looks very happy. There are not many of the latter, though. Rumor has it that there is danger up there above tree line without a car.

"I do not believe in persecuting the presidency over some second-rate burglary," L declares, slipping back through the oblivion to a popular daytime television series. "The entire episode is a creation of the Washington Post!"

"I liked him better before he became a bloody lawyer," Big Al laughs, reaching under his jacket and coming up with another aspirin. "Here you are, lad," he says, and drops it in L's open mouth like a mother robin.

A friendless-looking kid with long brown hair and Clorox-dyed cut-offs comes over and sits down in the shade beside us. He lets off his Sunbird pack and gasps with completion. He sits still for a few seconds waiting for someone to ask. No one does, and so he tells us.

"Whew. Been up there five days," he says, nodding significantly in the direction of a treeless ridgeline. "Good to be back down."

No one responds, but no one tells him to get lost, either, and he senses he is among friends. L hands him half a can of beer into which he has just dropped a cigarette butt. "Hey, thanks an awful lot," the boy grins.

"Don't mention it," L replies.

"Look, I … I've got this really terrific grass," he stammers after a few seconds, in the general direction of the People's Choice. "I thought maybe you'd want to buy some? It's really far out shit, I swear it is. Like, I could give it to you for, ah, I don't know, say twenty bucks for the bag? How's that sound? Like, I need the money to get home, you know? What do you say?"

"Weel, thet's greet fookin' news, in't it?" Big Al answers quietly, looking into his bottle of prune juice. "Boot whet's ta keep o' mon froom joost takin' yer fookin' grass, 'ey?"

The boy is amazed. His face falls like a curtain. He has come down from Nirvana and found himself in the third reel of a Peckinpah movie. For lack of knowing what else to do, he laughs.

"Come on you guys, look…"

"Joost how in the hell you know far sartin' I ain't soome kind o' bloody cop, huh?" Big Al cuts him off. "How'd you like it I turn oot ta be ol 'George FBI joost sittin' here an' waitin' far soome joonky poonk like yerself ta try an' turn a bloody bag on me, 'ey? How'd you like that?"

"I'll give you fifteen for it," the People's Choice says.

The boy's eyes dart past ours, searching for a way out. The closest people to him are the man and woman sitting at their table ten yards away. No help there. Intuition tells him he could probably make it to the road, but in a foot race he loses the pack, the grass, and the fifteen bucks. He hands over the bag to the People's Choice and collects his money. His soft hands tremble and there are tears in his eyes.

"Never thought I'd be getting ripped off out here," he whines.

"Thet's coontry livin' fer you in't it?" Big Al smiles.

The boy puts together his pack quickly, lifts it onto his shoulders and walks off shaking his head as he goes, hesitating every 50 feet or so and looking back. Big Al waves but the boy does not. He turns right along the road and puts out his thumb. A Volkswagen van stops and he gets in.

other and fold their hands to pray. . . .

"Honk your horn if you love Jesus."

Big Al rolls back, raises both legs, and farts.

We Plan a Climb

"Let's be gittin' after it then," Big Al says, coming back to the tree from the Jeep and carrying a wine carton filled to overflowing by the bulk of our mutual equipment. He drops the box between me and the People's Choice, who is just finishing his eighth beer and sinking back into a more comfortable time and space. There are two army surplus ponchos on top of the pile that we spread out on the ground for sorting and cleaning the gear. It is the first time we have seen any of it since putting it in the box nineteen days earlier.

Our preparations for this climbing trip had consisted of three phases, the first of which our Scottish mentor had described as base building. "The professional hae na need o' bein' taught how ta execute," Big Al had instructed us when we'd handed in our gear. "It is the state of his mind thet requires upliftin' an' spiritual preparation. Non climbing is the key!"

And for much of the last three weeks we had been non climbing like crazy. The first few days spent in Manhattan crawling back and forth on our hands and knees between the toilet and the kitchen in L's apartment were important in terms of our building a strong aerobic base, but were not ultimately satisfactory, according to Big Al. There had been a problem with concentration. I had claimed it was because we had never worked together before. L had blamed it on CBS and tried to rebuild his television set to receive transmissions passing through our solar system from other life forms, but he had only succeeded in setting fire to the east end of his living room. "We needs be closar ta thee moontains, boys," Big Al had explained, and shortly thereafter we'd all departed for New Paltz. Things had definitely gone better in the Shawanagunks. In fact it had gone excellently right up until we entered the second phase of our training. The "aggression" phase. One minute some local moron is making fun of Big Al's accent and the next thing anybody knows it's tables across the teeth, beer bottles over the back of the head, hard-toed boots between the legs, rolling in broken glass, and the band never missing a beat—what Big Al later chose to refer to as a very satisfactory indicator of our preparedness to climb. "Aggressiveness is a climber's stock in trade," he had said, pushing toilet paper into the hole in my forehead, "an' any mon who would hesitate to stick his fingers in another mon's eyes can be coounted upoon ta hesitate stickin' his fingers in a 2-inch jam crack with the bloody pressure on."

After that we went to Saratoga, because there was no place else to go and because the People's Choice said he knew a girl there, and to Bennington, Vermont, four days later to take L to see a doctor. Now at last we are within touching distance of Cannon and about to enter into the third phase of our training: the climbing phase. The afternoon we plan to spend polishing technique on some outcrops, get to bed early and tomorrow be up the scree by 6 A.M. to deal with a route called the VMC. As Big Al and I discuss the details, L rolls over on his side, holding his stomach with both hands, and moaning. Big Al smiles down on him with parental approbation.

"He's doone weel this week, the lad has," he says. "In fact, you booth hae. I think we're aboot prime!"

We begin untangling the ropes while the People's Choice plays in the runners where he is not in the way and of no danger to himself. Under a mixed bag of hardware and etriers he uncovers my sit harness.

Big Al grabs it, holding it up in front of him like a black leather garter belt, examining it closely.

"Queer, in't it?" he finally asks the People's Choice.

"Is the President really guilty of doing anything that hasn't already

"Lard help me Ja-sus," he groans to himself.

He reaches for his prune juice. L offers him another beer but he waves it away and rolls over on his stomach. For a long time the three of us sit curling into what shade we can find and watch wordlessly as the sunlight works across the face of Cannon and the couple beside us give new meaning to the word kinky. Later, L gurgles something down deep in his craw and between spasms of belching points in the direction of two people coming toward us. The girl is jogging, her gigantic breasts bouncing under a Dartmouth sweatshirt like two loaves of Boston brown bread. She drags her boyfriend behind her by the wrist. He is a wasted, nasty-looking kid, with huge, goofy hands fluttering on the ends of his arms like butterflies.

"In't it soomethin' though," Big Al observes, "the way o' wanker like him is always windin' oop with o' bird the like 'o her?" He shudders, thinks it over and then adds, "What the bloody hell. She's probably a fookin 'Hitler in the sack."

As the words come out of his mouth and the prune juice bottle goes back to it the girl looks at him, seems to hesitate for an instant and then comes directly toward him, pulling junior along with her. She stops 3 feet in front of Big Al.

"I'm sorry," she says softly. "I saw you were drinking prune juice. I...I wonder if maybe I could bum a hit off you?"

"Sure. Yes. Of course," Big Al replies, sitting up a little and holding out the bottle. "Help yerself."

"Thank you."

"Not at all."

She takes a few small sips. The three of us watch mesmerized. Then she passes the bottle to her friend. He drinks as if it is the first liquid he has seen in a month.

"Thirsty, in't he?" Big Al asks, trying to sound pleasant.

"Yes," she replies, watching him with a mother's pride, "he's always like that after we go hiking."

"Right," Big Al agrees, shaking his head. The People's Choice crawls around the tree, sniffing at it, then suddenly rolls over on his side and begins whimpering.

"Is he all right?" the girl asks.

"No," Big Al tells her, "boot he hae na been mooch bettar since I've knoown him."

"You're Scotch, aren't you?" she says.

"Scot-tish. Scotch is a drink, in't it?"

"I've been to Edinburgh," she replies with enthusiasm. "I thought it was one of the most beautiful cities I've ever seen."

"Yeah, weel I coome froom Glascow, you know."

"Oh. I haven't been there. I heard—"

"Yeah, yeah. I knew what yoou've heard," Big Al cuts her off. 'Course I'm noot there then anymore, am I?"

"No, I guess not."

Pause.

"I love prune juice," she says. "A lot of people don't, you know?"

"Not incloodin' yer yooung friend, there," Big Al responds. "Seems he has quite a taste for it himself. I'm fookin' pleased he wuz good enough ta relieve me o' it."

All eyes fall on her boyfriend.

"Hey, you guys climbers or something?" he asks, handing the empty bottle back to Big Al. The question seems to come to me and I nod my head. "You hear about those two guys that fell today?"

A Lot of Excitement

"Americans," Big Al says loud and angry enough to turn heads, "you make me sick to my fookin' guts." He spins and pushes his way through

posed to be looking for up

through the view-finders of home-movie cameras. The low level of conversation is continually punctured by waves of "ooohs" and "aaahs."

"In Scotland," Big Al mutters, staring away and leaning against an abandoned station wagon from Georgia, "they'd 'a hae 'em doon off o' there by new or at least they'd'a been so far froom a fookin' highway they'd'a nae had all these bloody fookin' ghoulies o 'watchin' 'em hang." He is cut off by sirens.

Two state police cruisers maneuver carelessly through the mob and stop at the ring of half a dozen other squad cars already on the scene. The officers get out slowly, adjusting their hats and basking in their importance and nodding to select members of the crowd. There is a man with them wearing a neat beige suit who has clearly overdosed on Efrem Zimbalist, Jr. He has a deep out-of-season tan, black Vitalis hair combed straight back, and the crow's feet around his eyes of a decision-maker. The crowd's attention swirls around him like a spotlight, and he gives them what they want. A miniature police walkie-talkie materializes in one hand, the other hand he stuffs down in a pocket, shoving his coat back far enough to show a corner of his blonde leather shoulder holster. More "ooohs" and "aaahs."

There are now perhaps twenty troopers on the scene, half of them standing around in casual daisy chains, arms folded over their chests, guns slung low on the hips, chewing gum, and looking out at the world through $26.75-a-pair aviator sunglasses. Others sit with their hats off in the front seats of their cruisers handling matched pairs of riot guns. Three or four, without the pull or seniority to stand around looking important, are out on the pavement directing traffic, keeping the public moving so that everybody gets a glimpse.

An ambulance arrives. The attendants get out and mix with the police officers. There is no rushing around after stretchers, no loud speakers or ladders. No one is talking about rescue anymore in terms of saving anybody's life. The man in the beige suit says the problem now is to get the bodies down without getting anybody else killed. He points up at the cliff for the attendants and everyone's eyes follow to where the two boys are hanging in a still pendulum from an overhang near the center of the main face. The unofficial report circulating through the onlookers is that they fell off 600 feet further up. The uh-oh voices say "gone off route and onto bad rock." Those with field glasses are talking excitedly about the bottom man and gore.

The People's Choice comes back from having offered our services with his head down and his hands in his pockets. "God, what a mess," he says, walking past us toward the Jeep. We fall in line behind him like ducklings. He climbs behind the wheel and starts the engine. "Let's go get a drink or something."

"I'm fer thet," Big Al agrees, "I can't bloody stand any more o' this."

We move out into the rubber-necking line of traffic and follow the road north to a motel on the edge of the park. From the picture window in the lounge we watch a group of people in tennis shoes and blue jeans with sweaters tied around their waists climbing an outcrop named Artists Bluff. The room is filled with tourists heading in both directions and stopping for lunch and a drink. The talk is about the accident and all very electric, those heading south and through the Notch trying to get information out of the ones going north. There is a rush on color film in the lobby.

"There were two other guys behind them on the route," L explains. "They were pretty shook, I guess. They both said there was no way anybody could survive a fall like that. The cops have been watching them for three hours and neither of them has moved. They're dead."

Silence follows; all the titillated prattle segues into Muzak, glasses clicking in the background, murmurs. We look into our drinks for a while,

wuz goin' ta be a manky rookin day, didn't i? i could j...
you know?"

In the lobby someone is on the phone to Boston and talking loud enough that his voice carries easily to the table. "Right, look I'll see what I can turn up, okay? I mean that's the best I can do for you, isn't it? Yeah, yeah, they're still up there, don't get all worried about that, for Christ sakes. The cops got someone coming to pull them off, I'll find out what I can then soon as I can corner somebody, all right? How the hell should I know who they are? Some college kids from down state, that's all I can get out of anybody right now. I'll let you know, quit worrying..."

He listens next, leaning against the cash register and dumping two handfuls of mints into his coat pocket when the girl behind the counter looks away. He is carrying two cameras around his neck, one the exact duplicate of Big Al's. He hangs up the phone after another moment or so without saying anything more, buys several rolls of Tri-X, and hustles out. We watch him jump into the call car of a local radio station.

"A lot of excitement around here today, isn't there?" the waitress asks cheerfully. "Will that be one check or three?"

"One," L says. "I'll take it, please." She finishes her calculations and puts the bill down on a small saucer. L lays a $5 bill down on it without even turning it over. A very classy person, this People's Choice, when he is sober. Outside, the scramblers on Artists Bluff have reached the top and are shaking hands, laughing and looking down on the scenery.

L grows desultory as we climb back into the Jeep. We discuss for a moment the possibility of going over to north Conway and climbing Cathedral Ledge, but the suggestion dies without interest. When he finds an opening, Big Al steers the Jeep out into the slow-moving traffic. We are hardly beyond the parking area at Echo Lake when the movement grinds to stop-and-go; by Boise Rock, where the two boys had signed in, all motion comes to a halt. The area is overrun with police cars, ambulances, a collection of National Park Service vehicles, and two trucks from a local academy filled with dozens of eager-faced schoolboys wearing orange helmets and wrapped in huge coils of goldline. They have come—apparently uninvited—to make the rescue and have been told no. The boys are openly disappointed, but their leaders seem to be the most upset and are standing in front of the trucks, bug-eyed and complaining to a handful of police officers who nod their heads without listening. The mob is pushing up around them to four and five deep.

As the Jeep pulls even with the main hub of activity and authority, there are more sirens and a small green-and-white Bronco comes through the crowd behind a highway police cruiser. Four very businesslike men in knickers get out and begin unloading their equipment as the man in the beige suit fills them in on the details. None of the four looks up at the face; they know the route and they have all seen dead people before. One of them is an Englishman with whom Big Al is vaguely acquainted. "He's very good, this fellow," Big Al says, "very professional." When the rescue climbers turn to walk into the woods the crowd parts before them like the waters of the Red Sea, filling in again behind them in a crush of newspaper reporters, policemen, and the curious.

A Karmic Ending

The traffic unplugs itself immediately after they disappear and before they have arrived on the scree we are turning into the entrance of the Lafayette Campground. The crowd there has thinned out considerably since the afternoon and has divided into those staying for the night, the kids heading for the Greenleaf Hut, and a few old sports booked into Holiday Inns somewhere who wouldn't have skipped Frontier Town to come up here in the first place if it hadn't had been for the accident. Our tent is standing unmolested beside the couple in the red Ford pickup, who are sitting at their table playing canasta and drinking iced tea. The

we have, by unspoken agreement, g

tomorrow. The vibes are not good. "Tuesday or Wednesday," Big Al says, "Wednesday, maybe Thursday. When the time is right, lads."

He is lying in his sleeping bag with his hands beneath his head, staring at the ceiling. His expression is sober and distant. Like most Scottish climbers, Big Al is a working-class boy. Brought up and educated after his parents' death by a long line of aunts and uncles, he was made a plumber's apprentice at fifteen and told that if the union would have him, and if he acted respectful-like, then just maybe someday he could move up and fill his old man's shoes in the shop. When he was eighteen, Big Al told his aunts and uncles what they could do with their plungers and went off to live in the mountains. Yet all of those growing-up years spent listening to everyone around him impressing upon him the need to settle down to a trade have had their effect. They have forced him to approach climbing as a job—something that, given a little hard work, a few late nights, and a year or two without vacations, a man could make his living at. But in the back of his mind it is the more heroic aspects of climbing that have made the greatest impression on his character. There are no promotions in being a professional climber and almost no money, but there is the possibility of immortality. The chance that by doing the first ascent of something no one has ever done before your name could go down in the guidebooks or in one of the magazines or, someday, maybe even on a plaque or something. In death climbers can often become bigger than they were in life. It is not a great deal, but it is more than an apprentice plumber looks forward to.

Of course the two dead boys and the crowd have added another possibility: the prospect of dying and becoming nothing more than a curiosity to people who don't understand. The People's Choice and I have other lives to go back to, but for Big Al this is all there is. He stretches out a little and unscrews the top of his last bottle of prune juice.

"Rootin' fookin' way o' dyin'," he says to no one in particular. He turns over on his stomach, drinks some of his juice. Then he reaches for the duffel bag. "Weel, one good thing coome of all this," he sighs. "We goot us soome good grass out of it, anyways."

He reaches inside the bag and withdraws the plastic sack and some strawberry-flavored papers. He opens the gummed wrappers and is about to roll a couple when he discovers there are already two rolled joints in the bag. "Weel, thet's bloody convenient, in't it?" he beams, withdrawing the two J's. He hands one each to me and the People's Choice. He rolls a third for himself. A roach the size of his index finger.

"Poot me to sleep, sweetheart," he murmurs, "Poot me ta fookin sleep." He lights it and lets his head back down on his arms, drawing in the smoke deep and holding it there. A look of perplexity crosses his face. Suddenly he is sitting up, hacking and coughing violently. When he can breathe normally again he looks at the joint, tears it open and examines it, then pours out the contents of the bag into the palm of one hand. He sniffs at it, puts a few twigs in his mouth and spits them back out.

"Thet skinny bostad!" Big Al roars. "The soon of a bloody bitch!"

Well beyond recognizing the solemnity of just having been ripped off for fifteen dollars and a lot of back-patting, the People's Choice begins to snicker. Somewhere in the depths of his stupor it all seems ridiculously funny to him. Big Al throws a glaring turn of the head at him, which only serves to set him off further. Now he is rolling on his back, holding his stomach with both hands and howling. One of his churning feet comes up and kicks Big Al's hand, spilling some of the phoney grass. Big Al reacts at first as if it were the real thing, then catches himself in his foolishness. He looks at the bag and then us. He throws what he is left holding at the roof and as it sprinkles down on us he begins laughing.

sudden presence inside our small tent comes as no great surprise. Big Al, who is nearest to them, sits up, flecks of the false twigs and seeds still spotting his long hair and beard. He holds out his arms like a crucifix.

"I knew you'd finally be catchin' up with us one o' these days, Hogan," he confesses to the officer crouching beside him. "It wuz oonly a matter o' time once we heard you wuz oon the job. I'd be guessin' this is as far as we've come, in't it?"

Officer Hogan stares down at Big Al as if trying to place his face on a post office wall. Behind him our next-door neighbor is staring around the tent, his face twisted with disgust. He is wearing blue-and-white striped pajamas and fuzzy bedroom slippers.

"All right, smart ass!" Hogan finally declares, "why don't you just start by explaining all that shit in your hair."

Big Al turns first to the People's Choice, and then slowly toward me. He snickers, and then the laughter begins again, rolling us under like a wave. All the absurdity of the last three weeks, the self-indulgence and over-the-top antics seem diminished to child's play in comparison to the insanity we have experienced in our brush with civil society. The rape of the land, the waste of wilderness, the mobs and media circus, and now the three policeman on their hands and knees in the front of our tent accompanied by the saliva-spitting wild man who only this afternoon we had watched humping his wife in the back of his Ford pickup, and who is now screaming, "See? See?" at the scattered remains of a plastic bag full of tea leaves, oregano, and catnip. Go ahead, Hogan. Arrest us. Maybe we deserve this. Maybe we don't. But then no one ever said it comes out even in the end, anyway.

PART V
Tales

FAT MAN

He was a blur, he was nothing, he was invisible, a rush of motion…a sight that haunts me to this day.

—T. Coragheessan Boyle, *The Human Fly*

The Fat Man appeared without a sound. Without luggage. Without the *deus ex machinas* of the dying. One morning he was simply there, lying on his back, his enormous stomach shimmering beneath blue and white hospital linens. Plump alabaster hands curled across his breast. Long gray hair fanning the pillow around his head. The Fat Man faced west toward the empty television screen.

Across the room, Michael Curtis pulled his knees up under his chin and passed much of the morning in contemplation of his new living arrangement.

Complaining would be of no use. Clearly, the Fat Man possessed the prerequisite morbidity to be on the eleventh floor. Neither did Michael's life insurance policy nor hospital procedure allow for him to live alone. The Fat Man was there to stay. A stranger full of questions bringing all his strange smells, weird relatives, and pushy doctors into his room. Worse, it meant being watched. Or, just as bad, having to watch. It seemed humiliating and unjust. An unnecessary loss of freedom. And yet, there was the Fat Man.

By mid-morning the sun had come out from behind a layer of rain clouds to sharpen the Fat Man's shadow. He began to moan. Just before lunch his wife came to visit. She had wide, sorrowful eyes, narrow shoulders, and an awkward, girlish shuffle. She was wearing a McDonald's uniform beneath her overcoat. The Fat Man waved one hand to her and she began crying. He pulled her head down on his chest and she wept like a heartbroken teenager, sobbing and coughing, banging the side of the mattress with her tiny fists. Her tears soaked the front of the Fat Man's pajamas. He looked over at Michael and blushed. A nurse appeared and led the Fat Man's wife out into the hallway. Michael never saw her again.

of his skin the Fat Man's heart began fibrillating like a dog in heat. He would have died right there on the table had his surgeons been less adroit. They split his chest like a wishbone and in so doing the Fat Man's life was saved but one of his lungs punctured. By the time they found the leak he had contracted pneumonia. Then he developed a severe infection, which resulted in the removal of his spleen, gall bladder, liver, and a large section of small intestine. Remarkably, it was after all this that things *really* began to deteriorate. A series of mysterious internal disorders cost the Fat Man major pieces of virtually every organ in his body. Finally, his beleaguered heart could take no more. It played its old stop-and-wobble trick again and this time the doctors told him he needed a replacement. Given the state of his general health, the Fat Man knew he was a poor candidate for a transplant. Time was running out. He could feel the coil tightening in the center of his chest. At fifty-one he had no expectation of ever getting out of bed again. "One day at a time," he told Michael. "That's all I look forward to. One day at a time."

Still, the Fat Man felt no bitterness. It wasn't anybody's fault. Sometimes things just happen. Why the folks back home had even taken up a collection for him, he laughed. Yep, they'd held a charity softball game in his honor and donated all the proceeds to, "A New Heart for a Great Guy." The Fat Man got tears in his eyes just talking about it. If he didn't make it, he said, the money would go to his wife. There was no sense in bearing any grudges. There had been no wrongdoing on anybody's part but his. He didn't intend to sue anyone. After two years of nothing but setbacks the Fat Man had settled comfortably into the embrace of fate. There was no pain anymore, he told Michael, and frankly after a life on the hustle the Fat Man had discovered that he kind of liked being waited on.

He showed Michael a photograph of his children. They were standing ankle-deep in the ocean: two tow-headed boys of about five or six years. They were squinting into the sun and wearing inner-tubes around their skinny stomachs. The Fat Man had another photo of his wife. She was sitting at a picnic table, smiling and holding a bottle of beer up to her cheek. Her eyes danced with brightness.

"So what's up with you?" the Fat Man asked, placing the two photographs on his bedside table.

"Same kind of stuff," Michael replied. "Pneumonia. Broken leg. A little frostbite." His voice tapered to a barely audible whisper. "I don't know. It's complicated."

"Too bad," the Fat Man sighed, shaking his head and taking a deep breath. "I'm sorry to hear that."

"It's okay," Michael told him. "It's not your fault."

The Fat Man raised an eyebrow. "No, I don't suppose it is," he replied, turning to look at Michael more closely. Then his eyes rose to the window. "Jesus!" he gushed, "Is that Mount Rainer out there?"

Michael answered without looking. "Yeah, that's it."

"Well, I'll be goddamned!" the Fat Man enthused. "That's great, isn't it?" Michael shrugged and picked up a magazine. "I used to read a lot about mountain climbing and stuff like that when I was a kid," the Fat Man explained. "I know it doesn't look like it, but I really would have liked to have been a mountain climber. It doesn't make much sense when you're a 225-pound twelve-year-old kid growing up in the desert. But that was me—always dreaming." He looked over at Michael and then back out the window again. "I don't read much anymore. Just the papers. I'm always reading the paper. I keep after the boys about books, though.

'Books are the difference between us and the monkeys,' is what I tell them. You never see my wife without a book. She's reading all the time."

His voice trailed off for a moment, as if something else had crossed his mind. Then he turned back to Michael. "You ever do any climbing?" he asked quietly. "I mean in the mountains and all that?"

way someone whistled the theme song to "Jeopardy." After a while Michael fell asleep and when he awoke again it was getting dark. He could hear the sound of traffic on the wet streets below. The Fat Man was still staring at the ceiling. There was a sheen of sweat on his upper lip. Long black hairs billowed out his ears. His eyes hardly blinked.

"I could tell you were sensitive about it," the Fat Man said, rolling his face toward Michael. "I used to be a pretty good salesman. A good sales-man knows people. Better than they know themselves, sometimes. Everybody wants to believe they're unique. But I'll tell you what—you meet enough people, you begin to get a pretty good sense of what they want you to think about them and what they're trying to hide. Hell, everybody's trying to hide something. That's part of human nature. People on this floor just aren't very good at it, that's all. No harm done."

Michael smiled and then fluffed up the pillow under his head. "So what am I trying to hide?" he asked the Fat Man. "What have you got on me?"

"Nothing," the Fat Man replied and then corrected himself. "Look, the way you got moody and everything when I asked you about Mount Rainier, that made me think you were some sort of climber or some-thing. I knew you didn't want to talk about it. The kind of injuries you've got. I put it together."

"And so?"

"So, I'm sorry. I should have kept my big mouth shut," the Fat Man apologized. "I didn't mean anything."

Michael nodded and turned on his back. "It's okay," he said. "I didn't think you did."

They lay in silence for a long time. Night settled over the city and rain beat against the window. In the great distance they could hear the rumble of thunder.

"You want to tell me about it?" the Fat Man asked.

"About what?"

There was a long pause. "Look," the Fat Man finally replied, "I'll tell you the truth. The doctors say I make all this stuff up. You know what I mean? They keep telling me that there's really nothing wrong with me. That's what I'm doing up here. Well, I don't know what to think about that. Maybe I am crazy. I don't know. But one thing I'm pretty sure of is that I'm not stupid. I read the papers. I knew I'd read your name somewhere. When you told me about being a guide I kind of put it together. You know, with your injuries and everything."

Michael nodded. "Nothing much to tell, really. You read about it. I don't know what happened."

"So why'd they put you up here?"

Michael shrugged.

They didn't talk for a while. Then the Fat Man rolled over on his side and reached under the covers. "Hey. You want something to eat?" He held out a handful of Tootsie Rolls and a Hostess Twinkie. "My wife sneaks 'em into me," he blushed. "I know they're not good for me, but hey! What's the worst that could happen, huh?"

Michael shook his head. "No thanks," he said.

The Fat Man ate happily for a few minutes then picked up the remote and turned on the TV. He watched reruns of M*A*S*H and Home Improvement, and laughed at all the jokes. At 6 P.M. he tuned in to World News Tonight with Peter Jennings. Then he turned the thing off.

"So when are they going to let you out of here?" he asked.

It took Michael a moment to realize he was being spoken to. "Oh, I don't know. When I'm better, I guess. When I'm dead. One or the other."

"Whew," the Fat Man whistled. Then he turned on his side and fixed Michael with his big sad eyes. "They all died, right?" he ventured carefully. "You were the only one who made it down?"

"Only me," Michael replied.

The Fat Man shook his head. "Man," he sighed in condolence. "I

...ng across this little hanging glacier to reach the last rappel set-up and he just disappears. I turn around and he's gone. I never heard anything, never saw anything. Just gone. I mean it was snowing and everything but God, it'd been snowing for weeks. I backtracked on my boot prints and found this hole in the snow. You could see where both of our foot prints led right up to it. Only I cross and he falls in. I laid down on the edge of it and screamed into the hole until I was hoarse but I knew it was pointless. There wasn't anything else I could do. After a while I went back to the rappel. It was a straight shot. We'd done it five or six times each. It wasn't anyplace you'd want to fall, but it wasn't technical or anything. But being alone all of the sudden I was trembling and crying the whole time I was setting up my rig. By the time I reached the glacier and the storm was getting worse and the spindrift was pouring down on me like a river and I'm thinking to myself, five guys gone and I'm the only one left and I don't have a dog's chance in hell. I mean getting through the icefall alone seemed like such a joke. The whole time I was walking I was wondering, Christ, what are people going to think? Nobody to tell our families. Nothing left of us but a couple beat-up tents. It never occurred to me that I'd make it out or anything. I figured I'd just go as far as I could. I must have fallen into fifty crevasses. One leg or the other. Sometimes both of them. I'd lay there panting. Waiting to fall, waiting to get my breath back. Waiting to live, waiting to die. It didn't matter to me one way or the other. Then I'd get back up to my feet and start going again. No route, no plan or anything. My eyelids were frozen half shut. I just zigzagged my way down. At one point I was so tired I just laid down and slept for awhile. When I woke up I was cold all the way down to my balls. I remember thinking, 'this isn't so bad,' and then just going back to sleep. I couldn't believe it when I woke up in the morning. It was almost disappointing. But I wasn't cold or hungry or sleepy anymore. I lay there for awhile and thought about things. It seemed kind of stupid to just sit, so I got to my feet and started walking again. Then after a while I realized I was getting pretty close to the toe of the glacier and with a little bit of luck it looked like I might be able to reach the lateral moraine. If I could do that it meant I could get to base camp, and if I could do that I could probably get home. And then all of a sudden it was like I was consumed with getting out and telling people what happened. I had to survive. Somebody had to tell them. I was the only one left. So I kept going. Of course the funny part is that when I finally did make it home I didn't know what to say. I didn't know how to tell people what had happened. Anderson's wife came to see me. What could I tell her? That we left him? That he begged us not to leave him and we left him? How could I tell her something like that? Or Craig's brother. He hung around for days waiting for me to get well enough to talk to him but I couldn't say anything to him. I couldn't say anything to any of them. Everything I had to say was so goddamn 'inappropriate.' What did I know about trying to make them feel better? So I just hid out. I crawled inside my injuries and stayed there. They were snipping off pieces of my fingers and toes back then, parts of my ears and nose, so I looked pretty forgivable. But later on it got harder. People started losing their patience with me. So I just decided not to say anything to anyone. Play the mad man. The mountain maniac."

Then he laughed. Just once. The hollow exhalation of a soul tearing itself in half. A laugh like suicide. The sanest and most miserable sound the Fat Man had ever heard.

"Jesus," he said. "You've been through the fucking mill, kid."

Michael smiled and rolled on his back. "Now you know," he whispered. "You're the salesman. You're good with words. You tell them."

Sometime later a candy striper brought in bed pans and dinner. Th

Fat Man whispered to Michael. "You telling me that little girl had never seen one before? Hell, with my blood pressure I'm glad I can still get one. She should have given me a pat on the head."

An hour later the nurse came back and turned the lights out. It was 10 P.M.

The Fat Man woke Michael a little after midnight. "I'm not feeling so good," he said. "It's like there's a fucking elephant standing on my chest or something." He was quiet for a few minutes, then added, "I feel like maybe my heart's beating too fast. It's pressing on me."

Michael called for the night nurse. She took the Fat Man's pulse and blood pressure. Michael asked her for a sleeping pill. He took it and then another that he'd been saving. The nurse left and it was quiet again.

"Tomorrow," the Fat Man murmured after awhile. "Tomorrow we should talk about letting people know."

"You're the man," Michael replied.

The Fat Man nodded and pulled at the neck of his pajamas. "Christ, it's hot in here," he muttered and twisted uncomfortably on his bed. "That's Mount Rainier out there, isn't it?" he asked.

Michael turned and looked at the window. The sky was black. The Fat Man was staring straight up at the ceiling. "Yep," Michael replied. "That's it."

"You ever climb it?"

"Yes. A long time ago."

"Someone told me once that they get 1,000 inches of snow a year up there."

"At Paradise they do."

"Yeah. I heard that, too. 'Paradise Lodge.' What a great name. Snows in August, doesn't it?"

"Sometimes."

"That's good. I wish I could have seen more of that kind of stuff. I mean nature and all."

"You will."

The Fat Man laughed and his laugh became a weak cough. "Yeah," he sighed. "Sure I will." He was talking to himself when Michael fell asleep. "Paradise Lodge," he heard the Fat Man say. "What a great name."

—

In the morning when Michael awoke his roommate's bed was empty. A set of fresh sheets had been folded neatly over a dark green hospital blanket. Clean pillows leaned against the metal headboard. The Fat Man's doctor stood in the hallway talking to a group of nurses. By noon they had wheeled in another victim. A young black man with a large scar on his cheek. It started raining. There were people in the hallways. They served pork chops for dinner.

FLESH EATERS

It shall be said that gods are stone.
Shall a dropped stone drum on the ground, Flung gravel chime?
Let the stones speak. With tongues that tell all t...

his arms hanging down at his side, palms up. Spindrift is gathering like dust on his thighs and in the folds of his jacket. His large head is back and up, his eyes open sightlessly, no longer even blinking away the flakes that land between the gray lids. The oval of his face is colorless. There are several long lines of ice dangling in broken chains from his moustache. Only his bottom lip is visible beneath it, a black scrawl drawn back into his mouth like rubber. Vomit glistens on his chin until it is absorbed by his beard. In back where his helmet is propped against the rock, his brains are seeping out of his broken skull and collecting in a wet sack in the hood of his cagoule. Lafferty has pulled the hood tight to the back of the Monk's head and wrapped it with an elastic bandage. It is the closest thing to first aid his frozen fingers would allow him to provide.

Mick Lafferty had invented the climb. It was his confidence that had brought the Monk here and placed him beneath the rock. But there is no blame, only coincidence; only the providence that saves one and sacrifices another. They had been standing side by side. Lafferty heard the rock first and screamed, but the Monk had moved in the wrong direction. The small boulder struck the back of his helmet and dumped him unconscious down on the ledge. Lafferty could tell by the sound of the impact—like a softball hitting a mattress—that there would be little he could do, but he had not understood the worst of it until he had placed his hand on the back of his friend's head to give him water. He had felt the splintered edges of the hole with his fingers then, and his hand had come away wet. His stomach had shrunk and turned over with horror and yet something—curiosity or concern, he did not know which—had made him slip a finger inside the Monk's balaclava and pull it away from the side of his head. Brain mixed with bits of blue wool, black hair, and pieces of white shining skull had slithered around the Monk's neck toward his ear. Lafferty then pressed the cap back against his friend's head and bandaged it. As he worked it occurred to him that they would both die on the ledge: the Monk very soon, possibly not until early morning for him. He accepted this calmly and finished his business, then coiled up the rope and made a seat out of it. Now that the excitement is over, the cold is beginning to settle on him. He no longer looks over at his friend's crushed head but pulls in close to him, drawing his feet up underneath his coat, leaning against him to absorb the heat. They tilt together like children away from the void.

By dawn the suspicion in the valley that they are in trouble has been confirmed. The excitement is almost tangible. Young men walk through the fog to Grant's shop where they stand around the stove in knickers and patched wind jackets, wearing boots half tied and talking quietly, intently. There is a rumor of a rescue attempt going around and they are volunteering by their presence. Not that they will all be able to go on the operation; what is important is that they will be close enough to it to later say they had been *there*. Coffee cups form them into small huddles, and outside there is the smell of early-morning marijuana. Jarold Grant, who runs the climbing school, is on the phone with Ron Tasker, who runs the park.

"Fish and Game," Jarold is telling him, "is just not up to something like this." The heads in the room nod and smile knowingly. But Tasker is unmovable. He has the bills, he replies, for having had his men trained by Jarold to be up to it. It is a hard line to argue and Grant is quiet as Tasker produces his paper proof.

Jarold's unusual silence spreads disappointment in the room behind him. It has been a slow winter and everyone wants very much to be in on this one. When he has his chance again, Jarold explains to Tasker in his press if something goes wrong. He agrees to two teams: four rangers and four local climbers, one group being lowered to the ledge and the other approaching by the icefall. Arrangements are quickly made for the air-lift, team leaders (Jarold, of course, and an ex-Yellowstone ranger named Ferthe), food, equipment, and camera teams. The local television station has asked permission to send along a crew and Tasker has attached them to the rangers. Jarold is too anxious to care about that now and quickly closes the conversation. He turns smiling to the climbers filling the room. No one claps, but there is applause in the air. Anticipation spreads like fervor as his face again turns serious. Almost as a single body the climbers seem to lean forward toward him.

"Fine-tune, goddammit!" Lafferty mumbles, his head jerking slightly. "I can't see a bloody thing for Christ sakes! Got to tune this damn thing in!" He searches the rock around him for the dials with his bare hands. His mittens have fallen off unnoticed and lie in the snow at the base of the ledge. He is not aware of any discomfort; his arms are dead now to above his elbows. He searches over the Monk, who is dead, too, and frozen hard. Lafferty does not know this. He no longer has any accurate memory of the Monk or the climb. He has entered the limbus, gone crazy with the cold and the slow work of dying, shrinking like plastic wrapping in a fire from the torment on the surface and drawing down to what little of the process there is left. Timeless gray light is on him. He sees images lurking in shadows, sees them moving, even recognizes a few, he thinks, and calls out to them, but they shrink back into the mist the closer he comes. "Fine-tune, goddammit," he grunts again.

~~

The rescuers are flown to the top of the mountain and lowered to the dead on a winch. Lines are attached to the bodies and they are lifted up the face like freight. An arm is lost. At the summit Lafferty and the Monk are packed in bags and taken away, nothing very dramatic. The team crossing the glacier is called back before they have even reached the base. Later, Jarold refuses Tasker's offer to come to the press conference and instead goes to the Snowcat Tavern with the others and gets very drunk. They drink boilermakers in silence as more people enter and gather at a respectful distance to form a ring of small whispering groups. The four climbers do not talk between themselves or to anyone else. They do not need to. The knowledge has already spread that they were the four who reached the bodies, the four who touched the dead. To discuss the event now would be to limit its proportions. At 6:15 the end comes when they all turn to watch Tasker on the news. He is dressed in his climbing clothes; he is very somber; he chooses his words carefully, almost wearily, seeming to think out the tangents before answering. It gives his statements a philosophical, climberly effect. He closes with a postscript on safety, his arms folded on the table and his mouth very near the microphones. When the television is snapped off Jarold leans back into single view from the table and shakes his head.

"What the hell does that son-of-a-bitch know?" he asks no one and everyone. "Hell, he wasn't there. He didn't know them. He didn't have to stuff them in bags for godsakes." Respect flows towards him like a river.

Time has passed. On the mountain it is a year now and snow has piled up in the Monk's corner until all that is left of his ever having been

two bodies wrapped in black plastic shrouds lying in the snow behind him. The same photo that now hangs in a wooden frame over the ice ax display in his shop. The photographer had given him a copy at Tasker's request. Perhaps to avoid any unkindness, Tasker's name had been left out of the article, but his television appearance had done him all the good he needed, anyway. In the spring he was transferred to Washington, D.C. and placed in charge of a study formulating policy on climbing safety in the national parks. Tasker wears climbing boots to work these days and is known to have seen the dead. For this he is greatly respected in our nation's capital.

LEVIATHAN

[It] is not unusual in human beings who have witnessed the sack of a city or the falling to pieces of a people to desire to set down in words what they have seen for the benefit of unknown heirs or of generations infinitely removed; or, if you please, just to get the sight out of their heads.

—Ford Maddox Ford, *The Good Soldier*

Kathmandu was cool and lush and muddy from the monsoon. The rail-thin Newar officials at the customs bench passed my bags along with an air of persecuted indifference and returned rapidly to their cold, white-tile offices, where they huddled in tight crowds around huge pots of tea on kerosene stoves. The odors of East and West mingled with the crowd in the airport lobby: leek and wool, deodorant and leather. The mistral wind gathered from the fields scents of jet exhaust and ox dung. I hired a hawk-nosed beggar standing near the gate to help me with my belongings and signaled for a taxi.

The city was crowded and busy, much the way I remembered Saigon. Instead of soldiers, though, there were Gurkha policemen wearing crisp khaki shorts, holding long, peeled switches and sharing street corners with sniffling Dutch junkies. Instead of *montagnards*, Tibetan refugees trotted to market in their red-and-black rags beneath enormous bundles of willow and alder twigs. Japanese taxis splashed the ooze and crap of the open sewers onto sidewalks and sacred cattle. Dogs lay dead and bloated in the streets. And I, Ishmael O'Brien (you can call me Izzy), found in the back pages of the *Alpine Journal* by an English eccentric, was once more a pilgrim in someone else's cause. In the thirteen years since my last visit to the Orient, the only thing I'd learned was climbing.

I took a room in the older section of the city at a hotel named the Kathmandu Guest House. There was an enclosed cobblestone parking area out front with a small restaurant off to one side. A yard in the back was furnished with white metal chairs and graced with parallel rows of neat Sussex gardening. The room had four beds and a large balcony overlooking the main entrance. The manager assured me that the beds

we approached the stairs. Then she smiled. "And good luck with the showers."

She walked quickly away from any possibility of a conversation, and I hiked my three leaden rucksacks up the steps. I dumped out everything onto the floor of the room and spent an hour separating my own things from the expedition equipment I'd brought with me. The sun came out and the cement steamed. The humidity sat in my lungs like water. I put on a T-shirt and nylon running shorts and stood at the window for a time looking out on the haze of the Himalaya with my mind full of autumnal Colorado.

After a short nap I ate a light supper in the restaurant outside the hotel and walked through the city to Freak Street in the European Bazaar. The evening light was golden and the air ripe with the odors of diesel exhaust and human waste. A small, wrinkled man in dirty cotton pajamas stopped me as I passed under an enormous lattice of bamboo scaffolds leaning against the side of an ancient temple. He took my arm and pressed a small plug of black hashish into my hand.

"If you like," he grinned, as harmless and beatific as Timothy Leary, "you come back."

I walked through the booths and stalls until dark, then climbed stairs to a second-floor coffee and yogurt shop. The owner was a Frenchwoman with vermilion hair and eyes that hung in her head like broken bulbs.

She brought me a bowl of sherbet with a mint leaf. With my spoon I crushed the hashish into paste against the table top and spread it on the sherbet. All around me names and phrases were carved into the wood in a babble of tongues. When I went back outside, my head was dancing like a trout on April water. I shuffled brainless and awed down side streets where naked twenty-five-watt bulbs backlit alley scenes as if Vermeer had passed this way on Quaaludes. I walked aimlessly along labyrinthine passages that smelled of urine and dry rot, buzzing in pot-head amazement of everything. I followed some poor, pumpkin-faced child who seemed to me to be rich with omen, but I lost him in a web of side streets. Passing ghostly ruins and a huge, ornately carved stupa, I came to a wide, bustling courtyard filled with night hawkers and fruit vendors. Along the fence stood God's occasional mishaps, laughing and gossiping and swinging deformed arms or legs swollen with elephantiasis and occasionally calling "Baksheesh, Sahib? Baksheesh?" One particularly capitalistic dwarf stepped directly in front of me, poking out his hand and forcing a perpendicular grin. His head was tilted sharply against his shoulder and the whole of his face and thorax—from skyward ear to waist—was a single mass of featureless skin. No clavicle, no breast, no separated arm: just melted, homogenous flesh. An unfinished man; an act of staggering cosmic felicity. I studied him for some time, then shook the outstretched hand, thinking to myself that, no, this was indeed not Boulder. I had come a long way on the strength of a voice over the phone and a ticket in the mail.

Two days later, on 11 October, two of the others arrived. I met them at the airport and helped them pass through customs. They had met for the first time in Delhi but weren't able to sit together on the crowded flight to Kathmandu. I had no difficulty, however, in picking them out from among the other passengers.

Hamish Frazier was robust and heavyset, with a great, ginger-colored beard that flew loose at his temples and thinned to premature baldness atop his rosy, weathered head. His woolen shirt, tucked carelessly into baggy trousers, barely restrained his huge chest and shoulders.

For a climber he had a surprisingly large paunch; for a Scots mountaineer he looked absolutely right. I liked him immediately.

Metilkja Martincz was a different sort altogether. A European hard man, he was taller, very dark, and somber. He seemed broodish—tender, angry, and contemplative. His hair hung in a tousled mop, his

visa and visit some old acquaintances.

"Fookin' pigsty, this place, eh, Jimmy?" Hamish enthused as we sped toward town. "Third time I've been here and I'll be boogery if it smells any better. It's the fookin' cows, ye know, lad? Aye, ye can't have 'em muckin' about the fookin' kitchen without expectin' 'em ta draw flies now, can ye?" Then, turning back to me, "Where ye got us puttin' up ta doss, lad? The Kathmandu?"

I nodded, somewhat disappointed.

"Right as fookin' rain, then, Jimmy! I imagine there's the usual lack of available quim standin' by, right? It's a long goodbye on that, these voyages, in't it, laddie?" He laughed ironically for a moment and then turned to watch Kathmandu arrive. After a time he looked back at me, suddenly more serious. "When's the Major sneakin' inta town?" he asked, as we careened around a corner, scattering shoppers. "I'll bet a pint he dinna tell ye, now, did he? He's a bit queer for surprises, that one."

He paused, seeming to think that over, then started in again. "Fook, I'm hoongry. That wee spot next door still there? Bit dear, I thought, but the woggies cook a potato right. What sort of name did you say Ishmael O'Brien was, anyway, lad?" On and on like that, episodic monologues, almost all of them rhetorical, and less than half, I suspected, meant to be heard.

We hauled the gear upstairs and spent the rest of the afternoon dividing it into two dozen separate piles. "I've a wee taste, O'Brien," Hamish finally concluded. He looked tired from the long flight and the heat. We put on clean shirts and went downstairs to the Star Restaurant. The Nepali owner showed us to a table in the corner beside the woman I had met a few days earlier. "'Ello, Sheila," Hamish muttered in a shammed Australian accent as we took our seats. She never lifted an eye, just kept to her book and tea. Hamish rolled his eyes and ordered six beers.

I had expected him to be more aggressive, louder as a drinker, but mostly we sat in silence. We both drank our first two bottles before he even spoke. He asked if I'd ever met the Major. I said, no; in fact, I knew very little about the man. Hamish looked at me doubtfully, almost angrily, for an instant, then switched his gaze to the room.

"Well, don't you be believin' everything you hear, O'Brien. He's all right. A bit odd, maybe, boot who isn't a bit queer comin' on these fookin' crusades, eh? Aye, you get caught up in somethin' like this, spendin' your money, dear as it is, to take a whack at killin' yerself for ten minutes o' standin' in the wind on some nameless mountaintop. Vicar's tits, mon, it'll make ye a bit funny, then, won't it?"

He was silent again for a moment, searching for the right words.

"You rich, O'Brien?"

I told him no.

"Major's rich as fookin' Croesus, I reckon," he said. "Probably crazier than a fookin' Cumbrian goose, too, for all I know about behavin' in public. But I kin tell ye this. He's a right hard man to have with you on a piss-up, strong and steady as any I've ever seen touch ax to snow. Aye, game as they come and a straight man with ye, too. The type that'll see ye through a shitstorm without a word."

We sat quietly for a while. We each ordered another bottle of beer and Hamish got a sandwich. I asked him if he knew much about the mountain or the route. He said no, only that the Major had taken a close look at it the year before during his solo attempt. Some people, he added, were saying the usual thing about its being the hardest thing attempted at that altitude. The Major had spent two and a half weeks on it by himself, he explained. No food at the end, bad weather, and, for a while, not much hope of getting down alive.

"Lost his mind up there, I suppose," Hamish said without emphasis or lifting his eyes from the remains of his sandwich. "I reckon he thinks

It took a moment before it occurred to me that she had spoken. The atmosphere around her had been so hard I didn't imagine it could be talked through. When I turned, she was facing me, smoking a small cigarette wrapped in brown paper. She was impossibly beautiful. I was stunned and a little drunk and desperately in love.

"Yeah," I stammered, trying to sound urbane and casual. "We're a mountaineering exped—"

"Right," she cut in, "the Kahli Gurkha bunch. I know. The southwest face, I believe?" I nodded and she went on. "The Leviathan—or something like that. Isn't that what you're calling it? Much better name than the Nepali one, I'm sure. Probably bloody hard to go about raising money to climb a mountain with a name the bankers in London can't pronounce. 'The last great problem,'" she mused cynically. "Get you laid back home, mate?"

I was shocked dumb. Titillated and overwhelmed.

"Look," she semi-apologized, "I work for the Sherpa Cooperative. I get all this shit across my desk season after season. Every year it's someone off to tame the hardest mountain, the worst route, the steepest face. Christ, our records are like obituaries of who's-been-who in the Himalaya for the last twenty years. The young and the starry-eyed off to get themselves killed for the greater glory of European alpinism, and usually taking a few Sherpas with them. Hoo-fucking-rah, mate. I haven't seen a bloody Yank over here with his head on right yet, and you're just the same as the rest of them."

"Thanks," I grinned. I think I grinned. I tried to grin.

"Oh, look…. I've offended you; I'm sorry." She smiled and seemed to slow down for a moment. "Listen, I'm a bit off, I guess. I don't mean to come down like your bloody Mum or anything. It's just that I've seen this same act repeated so many times since I've been here I get the feeling that somebody ought to step in and say something, whether it changes anything or not!" She caught her rising frustration this time and sat back with it against the bench. She shook her head and smiled. I wondered if she could hear my heart beating.

"'One climbs to know oneself,'" she recited, "'and in so doing at last comes to know nothing. The being has been no more than the doing.'" She lit another cigarette, cupping her hand over the flame and letting the significance settle. "Does that mean anything to you at all?"

"Sure," I shrugged. "I guess it does."

"I knew it wouldn't," she replied after a pause. She smiled again and exhaled smoke into an atmosphere thick with the satisfaction Westerners seem to derive from the mastery of the enigmatic Zen parable.

"Do you know what a *chod* is?" she asked next. I shook my head no. "It's a tantric rite whereby the true believer commits himself to encountering his worst fears. A monk, for example, who finds he is frightened of the spirits he believes to inhabit a graveyard will spend a night meditating in the graveyard. Defeating fear: meeting the dragon and finding out that it is only air, the creation of his own imagination. I nodded my head, anticipating the lesson. "That is why you—climb. Because you are afraid to. It is your *chod.* "

"My mother will be crushed," I told her. "Quitting college was one thing, but if I turn into a monk, it's going to kill her." I smiled and she did not.

"The monk cleanses himself," she continued. "He goes expecting nothing and thus is prepared to accept everything. He empties himself of ambition. You, on the other hand, are not going to the mountain— you are going to the summit. Even if you succeed, you fail, because you never left New York or Iowa or wherever you're from. You just brought it

smoke and leaned closer.

"Look, don't be daft, will you. Your Major. I've heard the Sherpas talk about him. None of them will work for him. You know that, don't you? They call him a *sennin*, a bloody mountain lunatic! That's why he's had to go ahead to Khandbari to find people. No one in Kathmandu will—"

"Look, lady," I cut her off, "I appreciate the introduction to Zen 101. I'm sure everything you say is absolutely true." She started to speak, but I held up my hand. "Honest to Buddha, I don't know what the hell you're talking about. I'm afraid you've got the wrong guy. I'm just good old time-flogging Izzy O'Brien, and all I'm doing over here is going to climb a mountain. No spiritual mission, no ghosts or anything; just see the sights and do a little climbing. You can read whatever you want into that, I guess, but where I'm concerned, that's all there is to it." She started to speak again.

"That's it," I almost shouted. "I'm sorry; I'm just not that complex. Christ, I thought *chod* was a frigging fish or something." She laughed over that one. She let her head fall back, and her wonderful breasts vibrated beneath her leotard. I grinned, feeling stupid again.

"Look, mate," she said finally, "I'm awfully sorry. Your pie is getting cold." We both laughed until the mood seemed better. "My name is Lucy," she added, sticking out her hand for me to shake. "Tell me, O'Brien, do you abuse drugs?"

We said goodnight on the steps below her door. She put her hand on the side of my face, but I made no effort to kiss her. I was beyond arousal—drug-sodden, bewildered, strangely mordant. I listened to her door close and went out onto the balcony. It was 3 A.M. and the city sighed. Its potpourri scent and amber lights lolled on breezes that rustled the palm fronds in the garden. Fred Astaire would have danced. I just wove awkwardly toward our room and slipped quietly through the door, threading mounds of gear.

Hamish was in the far bed, snoring and gagging in perfect tranquillity. I took off my shirt and trousers, Lucy still cartwheeling through my brain, and slipped under the sheets on my bunk. There was a grunt—distinct, sleepy, and very near—and an unexpected contact with skin. I dove out of bed yelping "Jesus!" and rolled sideways along the floor. Behind me the entire surface of the bed seemed to rise. I collided heavily with a rucksack and struggled wildly to get the ice ax off it.

"That'd be Metilkja, lad," Hamish explained sleepily. "Bonnie great booger he is. Aye." Then he drifted back into sleep. The Yugoslavian sat smiling as I circled warily to the next bunk, ice ax in hand, trying very hard to seem collected and poised.

"Goot day," he said pleasantly.

"Good day," I told him.

In the morning we went to work on the gear heaped on the porch, dividing, listing, and crating the food, tents, clothing, climbing equipment, and personal belongings into eighty-pound loads. We packed the loads into plastic garbage cans and covered them with burlap sacks. For $2 a day a porter would carry one of the loads plus his own food and shelter. Lousy union, but they were still known to strike on occasion; so we were giving away sunglasses, tennis shoes, socks, and mittens. We also had cheap wind shirts, with "Leviathan" emblazoned on the back, packed away for extra commercial leverage later on, should it become necessary. We worked steadily and without much conversation. The sky was clear, and the cement floor reflected the tropical heat at us. It was the first hard work of the trip. Our T-shirts darkened with sweat. Metilkja played depressing Croatian symphonies on his tape recorder. We dragooned a number of gleeful children into fetching pot after pot of tea for us. Hamish referred to the process as the British colonial touch.

By mid-afternoon we had tied off the last package. Twenty-six plastic garba

"Right, well, I reckon starvin' is probably goin' ta be our last fookin' worry on this whale hunt," Hamish laughed. "Puttin' up the route is goin' ta be the hard part."

"Alpine met-tod," Metilkja concluded. "Goot weather, we climb fast." That seemed to me to be about the beginning and the end of it. Get and go; what else could you say? Not enough food or rope to stick it out for long, anyway. "If you want to last, you got to go fast," was the expression we had used in Yosemite. No pain, no gain.

We all took cold showers—the hot water was mythical—got into our best clothes, and went out on the town for supper. The three of us and all our gear were scheduled to be flown out in the morning, and the atmosphere of celebration was dampened only by the question marks surrounding the Major's absence. Behind the laughter was the lingering sense that he was already on the expedition and we were holding him back, slowing him down. I think we all had the feeling of wanting to show him we were as committed and hungry as he was, which was probably just the way he wanted us to feel.

We walked back through the city in the last light. Kerosene stoves burned in the small shops and market stalls; rice and lentils and black tea boiled in tin pots. People were bustling past us on foot and pedaling bicycles. A water buffalo lay on its side in the street, legs bucking spasmodically as its freshly decapitated head was raised through a haze of flies to a butcher's bench. Rich, crimson blood pumped into the gutter. The same dull lights threw yellow halos around every act of love and antipathy. Turning to take the unpaved alley that led down to the guest house, we passed a beggar lurking in the shadows behind the wreck of a Datsun taxi. He crept out into the dirt behind us, crouched over slightly to one side, thin and tattered, a crude bamboo crutch held under his right arm. He was wearing the emaciated remains of what had once been a down parka. We had never seen a beggar so close to the guest house, and his appearance caught us by surprise. Hamish took a threatening step toward him, and the beggar cringed back pathetically.

"No, Sahib! Please no, Sahibs," he pleaded, bending even lower to emphasize his terrible harmlessness. "Sahibs go Kahli Gurkha, please?" he asked.

We looked at each other. Hamish answered, "Aye."

"No go, Sahibs. Very bad, you go. Not good mountain. Masta go Kahli Gurkha. Avalokita Ishvara not go that mountain. Cannot see Sahibs. Masta live mountain. Sahibs go back America, please!" His voice broke with a sob. He paused and caught his breath. When he began again, his voice seemed to have changed, to have risen an octave. "Baksheesh, Sahibs? Baksheesh?" His shriveled, cupped hand stuck out at us from his rags.

"G'won git, ye wee fookin' chough!" Hamish scowled and turned to join us. The beggar dodged off into the darkness, and the three of us walked back to the guest house in a profound and insulated silence.

~~

We flew east. The valleys dropped away below us to isolate small hamlets on hogback ridges. No roads marred the landscape. I had been told in Kathmandu that atavistic Hindu sects still conducted human sacrifices in villages not 40 miles from where commercial jets disgorged loads of camera-toting tourists on high-adventure tours of the world's most remote region. To the north, the Himalaya lay in the dense cloud cover of monsoon season.

We landed on a grass runway with a miniature stucco terminal topped by an unattended bamboo control tower. A complement of police, militiamen, traders, and the curi̶ ̶ ̶ ̶ ̶ ̶ ̶ ̶

̶ ̶ ̶ ̶ ̶ ̶ ̶ ̶ ̶ ̶ ̶ ̶ ̶ of piain trees. Everywhere, small Buddhist prayer walls and tiny stupas were decorated with brightly painted mandalas and symbols. It began to rain after we had walked an hour or so. We unfolded our umbrellas and stopped by a rickety tea shop for *chai* and cookies. A Nepali child watched us drink. Her mother brought us bananas, for which Metilkja arose and thanked her with a deep bow, sending her giggling uncontrollably back into a corner. Her husband, a withered and tough-skinned old man, brought out his faded ledger. It showed that he had carried for several expeditions going into the Makalu area. We nodded. He smiled and came to attention, saluting. "Ed-mund Hil-lary," he pronounced carefully.

We arrived at the guest house in Khandbari around five. Ang Phu had caught up with us and showed us to a room with five or six straw pallets where we dropped our light trail sacks and went downstairs to join Major Abrams. He had arranged a side room for dinner and met us at the door.

⎯

The Major was a tall, lean, dark-haired man in his late forties or early fifties with sunken cheeks beneath a heavy beard, surprisingly narrow shoulders, and an awkward, almost feminine dimension to his posture. Much to my surprise, he walked with a marked limp, one leg being noticeably shorter than the other, though he was obviously not crippled.

His squinted eyes threw out deeply weathered crow's feet around the most intense glare I have ever seen. His presence was commanding, whole and authoritative; there was a cool, almost military ferocity about him that made calling him Major far easier than using his Christian name.

He shook hands with all of us. A solid, measuring grip. "Ah, Mr. O'Brien! The American," he grinned. "Good, you've got long hair. Something to pluck you out of the crevasses by!" We all laughed. As we took our seats around the table, I thanked him for his help and for the photos he had sent me.

"I'm afraid I really haven't been much help at all," he apologized, "but you're welcome, and I thank you for the compliment. As you all know, things have been very difficult trying to put this trip together on short notice. Lost paperwork, troubles with permission, the usual Nepal muck-up. Didn't give me much time to help you lads at your end, I regret to say."

We all assured him that things had run very smoothly for us, largely owing to his efforts, and that we all were keen for the climb. He asked pointed, knowledgeable questions of each of us as we ate. Occasionally he would jot down a note or pause with his head back, studying a response. He seemed warmer and more accessible than I had dared imagine. I thought of Lucy's Buddhist hyperbole and nearly laughed out loud.

After we were done eating and everyone but me had produced a pipe, the Major ordered *chang*. It was served hot, in tall bamboo gourds. It smelled richly alcoholic and was the color of milk. Seeds and rice and bits of leaves floated in it innocently. "To Kahli Gurkha," the Major smiled, raising his gourd. "To the Leviathan. To us."

We raised our *chang* after him. "To the Leviathan."

In the days that followed we hiked along the single spine of a long, fertile plateau. The Arun River lay to our left, gray and floury with the silt of unseen glaciers. On our right the terraced fields were black and ripe. We bought potatoes, carrots, and radishes along with an occasional chicken to supplement our trekking diet of rice and *tsampa*. The Nepalis we met on the trail were tolerant and friendly, although at night when we set up camp near their villages the aggressive mobs of curious on-lookers made us feel tense and militant.

Ang Phu had hired an assistant, a bull should

first sun touched the tents, a cup of tea and a warm *chapati* came through the front flap at the end of a square, brown hand.

None of the rest of us were particularly gregarious; perhaps the Major and I the least. Hamish could be loud and obscene, and he and Metilkja would walk together from time to time; but by and large we traveled alone on the trail. We carried simple lunches of candy and biscuits in our pockets. Sometime around midday I would stop at a tea shop, sit at one of the tables, and shout *"Namaste!"* to the porters as they came by under their huge loads.

The whole experience for me was an ongoing vision of incredible poignancy and beauty, intensified by my solitude. Images of magnifi-cent pulchritude were framed by even greater scenes of almost hallucinatory splendor. I stood in awe of every hut, every rhododen-dron, every detail. It was a walk like a dream, a fantastic trot. I watched huge leeches quavering at attention from the ends of trailside leaves, with tropical wildflowers setting off their grotesque dance in a dazzling profusion of colors and shapes. The sun rose out of the high jungle above Darjeeling and set in the forbidding aridity of the Kampa Mustangh. I took my time and exposed roll after roll of film. I crouched underneath my umbrella during the afternoon showers and wrote long, jovial letters to Lucy and my family. I wrote about the mountain as if it were the Panama Canal: a place one sailed through, not where people worked and died. I was very brave in print, of course, incapable of even alluding to the possibility of death. There, in the jungle, far away from the wind and snow, I was immortal.

We dropped down from the last Nepali villages, crossed the Arun on a primitive hemp-and-cable bridge, then hiked uphill for a day to the village of Sedua. For the Khumbu Sherpas it was like a voyage backward through time to what Namche Bazaar must have been like before it was "civilized." We called it Dodge City, guarded our baggage carefully, and moved on as soon as we could.

The days grew colder and clearer. We climbed steadily. At Shipton Col I caught up with the Major; he was standing alone, above and to the right of the trail, his piercing eyes fixed on the northern horizon. We were at 14,000 feet and it was cloudless, perfect. Makalu, the fifth-highest mountain in the world, stood out spectacularly. Just to its east I saw Kahli Gurkha. It seemed small by comparison, but even at this great distance its awesome southwest face—the Leviathan—stood out in startling relief. Illuminated by the southern post-monsoon light, it shone bronze- and sepia-colored with a blue-white fin of ice along its spiral summit ridge. As Abrams stepped down, his lips were moving wordlessly and his fists clenched so tight the knuckles seemed ready to burst his skin. He strode away from the crest and off toward the Leviathan in silence.

Supper was quiet that night. For the seventh consecutive night we shoved rice and *tsampa* around our plates without much enthusiasm and went to our tents early. Sometime after midnight I got up to urinate and stood for a long time in the moonlight looking down into the Arun Gorge. It was dark as dirt down there, but I could hear things bumping around: rock and mud shifting to the downbeat of eternity. The breezes that rose off the river carried sighs from the center of the earth and stirred the sides of our nylon houses. I listened for a long time. Then, walking back to my tent in the metallic light, I heard a cry of such private horror that it stopped me in my tracks. A scream in awful counterpoint to the pleistocene sonata issuing up from the gorge; torment of such grandiose scale that it could utter no words or name. I knew, of course, that the dreamer was Abrams, and that his photos had told me far less about the mountain than his nightmares did now.

⌐⌐

....u.. v.icu in dense clouds, and we neither spoke of it nor looked in its direction. It was there; that was enough to know.

We broke into our best food and had a superb dinner of beef stew with potatoes and barley. The Major produced a can of pears and a large gourd of a Nepali liquor called *rakshi*. For the first time in several days the conversation that night was animated and crude. The Europeans smoked their pipes and talked about climbing in the Alps. I went outside and dug into the small traveling stash Lucy had given me. I stood beside the river taking long draws and feeling the snow wet my face.

The snow fell steadily for a week. Avalanches sloughed off the peaks around us and roared unseen above the low-hanging clouds in the valley. We sat inside and waited. We killed time reading, writing letters, and playing with our equipment. I hung one of the single-anchor bivouac platforms in the branches of a poplar and watched the Europeans struggle with the notion of sleeping suspended in it. They, in turn, grinned at my lame enthusiasm for the cans of bacon and kippers they included in our climbing rations. We packed it all into our rucksacks along with rock climbing gear, ice screws, pots, and stoves, then for a week we lifted, weighed, divided, and revised our loads. Hamish built a sauna out of willow wands and our tent flies. We would sit in it until the sweat exuded from the soles of our feet, then run and jump naked into the frigid Arun. The Sherpas loved it. They would always gather to watch the spectacle and laugh hysterically.

During the sixth day the snow came down heavily. By noon we were sitting in the hut, idle as monks, and listening to the almost constant rumble of the avalanches above us. We warmed our hands on teacups. The Major sat in a corner smoking his pipe and writing in his journal. An unusually loud, baritone roar drew all eyes to the ceiling. "That ought to clean the face," Hamish mumbled. The noise grew nearer and deeper. The ground shimmied. Our eyes came down to meet one another's. Outside we could hear Ang Phu's excited voice and the other Sherpas shouting. Pots and pans began falling.

"Ja-sus fookin' Christ!" Hamish suddenly bellowed. "It's comin' right fer home!"

We leaped simultaneously to our feet and pushed each other through the door, bounding miraculously through the kitchen without knocking over steaming pots, hitting the clearing on the run, and splitting in three separate directions. The ground quaked, and the shock wave blew snow horizontally at our backs, though by the time I had reached the trees at the riverbank the slide had lost its momentum in the talus breaks above the hut. I stood against a tree to catch my breath, watching the air clear. The main tongue of the avalanche had reached to within 100 feet of the shack. A few small boulders were still rolling on the debris-strewn lower surface of the slide as Hamish approached.

"Christ's eyes, eh, laddie?" he laughed, wiping mud off his sweater. We walked back together. Metilkja and the Sherpas approached from the opposite direction. Metilkja explained with surprising seriousness that he took this to be a sign, that someday one of these was going to catch up with him. For all the noise of a few moments earlier, there was now an incredible stillness. Effort and release.

The Sherpas set to reconstructing the kitchen, and the three of us ducked back into the hut. The low door on the side of the building facing the mountain was open. Abrams was standing outside, some distance away, smoking his pipe, hands in pockets, and staring up at the Leviathan as it appeared in glimpses caught through the swirling clouds.

Snow powdered the ground between where he stood and the hut, but I saw no trace of footprints. He had been there when the snow came. He had walked toward the avalanche, not away from it. It had stopped at his very feet.

The next morning dawned spectacular......

......placed it in a small plastic satchel hanging near the door. He tapped out his pipe and stuck it in his shirt. His face was set and hard. This was it, the point of it all, and I couldn't imagine any human being with whom I would rather have gone up on the mountain. Abrams had the power. You could feel it in everything he did that morning. His obsession was like a magnet, a beacon. I was amazed at my own fanaticism. The pointlessness, the triviality and expense, the whole dramatic absurdity that underlay our climb struck me at that moment as the most important purpose my life could ever have.

The Major stood and stretched. "Well, lads," he said, his quiet voice suggesting neither a question nor command. The three of us rose and he nodded.

"Major-Sahib!" Ang Phu called from the kitchen. "Mens coming Makalu. Four, maybe five. Come down valley very near now, Sahib!"

We followed Abrams through the door and saw the men emerging from the trailhead at a willow thicket. They looked grim, bent on a mission of importance and solemnity. The snow sparkled in the sunlight and crunched beneath their huge boots. The Leviathan, cut from the cobalt sky, stood massively indifferent to our meeting. Waiting.

We all shook hands. Their leader explained that they were Dutch, part of a team attempting the south face of Makalu. Tears welled suddenly in his eyes. One of their members, he said, his son, the expedition physician, was missing. He had gone out of one of the tents at high camp two nights earlier and simply disappeared. They wanted our help to search for him. It was two days' travel to their base camp; the search would last no more than a few days, then they would give up. We could be back in a week at the most.

Abrams never blinked. He never paused to search for words. "You are welcome to food and tea here," he said. "You may take our Sherpas to help you if they are willing to go with you. Ang Phu, there, is a fine mountaineer, as competent as any European, I assure you. But we did not travel this far to lose hold of our goal because you have lost yours, sir. I shouldn't ask that of you, gentlemen. I'm sorry. That's final. I hope it all comes out well for you. I wish you good luck and godspeed. Good morning, gentlemen."

He turned and walked to his pack, brought it up onto his shoulders, and started toward the glacier. Less forcefully, the three of us fell in behind him.

"It is you I feel sorry for!" the leader of the Dutch party screamed after us. "I pray that you will find the same charity on your mountain that you have shown us, Abrams!"

The Major did not recoil or turn around upon hearing his name. It was hard to tell if he was even aware of its having been said.

⚊

We climbed steadily throughout the day. The going was not technically difficult, and we found the heat to be more of a problem than the crevasses or icefalls. At noon we stopped and took out the ropes. As the angle increased, the snow became wet and heavy. We sank in to our knees and ran short of breath beneath our monstrous loads. We dug a platform into the side of a crevasse and spent a comfortable night. The incline and mire increased all the next day. We reached the bergschrund where the lower glacier fractured at the base of an 1,800-foot ice face and carved out another small platform. We melted snow for tea and tried to make sense of what rose above us. The scale was out of proportion

as infinity. Under a muted afternoon sun I had filled its cracks with my hands and feet, twisting and panting, moving quickly, charged by my own elation and energy. The clouds moved in time-lapse speed and snow began to fall—fat, star-shaped flakes. My cheeks and hands were moist. I drove a piton when the rope ran out and raised the haul sack before descending, breathless, back down to the cave, whispering "In the morning" to myself.

The snow fell finer and harder the next day. The crack turned rotten, then disappeared altogether, leaving me swinging from sky hooks with the sweat stinging my eyes. I lost hours drilling holes for lousy bolts. Pitons I had hammered barely past their tips creaked and moved under my weight. I begged Jesus/Buddha, please, just ten more feet. My scrotum shrank in tingling cowardice. Scared to death of where I was and too frightened to go back down, I held my breath and swung on a rotten flake lassoed from 30 feet away to reach for a huge, fragmented block. Around more corners the angle of the face dropped to less than vertical and the cracks were filled with ice. I climbed to a large ledge and secured the ropes. Fewer than 300 feet for the day. Abrams prusiked the fixed line to join me and we hauled the sacks. His face was contorted with impatience. He knew he couldn't have done it any faster, but he hated to depend on others, on me, to wait on the expertise and judgments of fools. It dawned on me that he did not climb out of love for the climbing. That had passed long ago. It was out of hate for the mountain, for its superiority, its naked power. And strangely, I admired that in him, wished that I could have his ruthlessness. I was his vehicle, I knew, and he could drive me faster. I would give him his snow ridge.

Early the next morning, our fourth on the mountain, we climbed the ropes to the ledges we were now calling the Hilton and pulled up our umbilical line. To get down now would mean getting up. It seemed like a significant moment; yet it passed without anyone giving it notice. The inclination of the rock continued to ease. I climbed quickly now, rope length after rope length, one boot on rock, one on snow, my mittened hands jammed between dank shelves of granite and rivulets of ice. The snow fell quietly, relentlessly. Occasional breaks in the clouds let the sun through, and the rock steamed. We moved steadily up. When I leaned out to study the route, I could see the long, white tongue of snow above us: the Whale's Tail.

The day ended with the four of us suspend...

...the rock was not steep enough to hang our nylon platforms; so we chipped out whatever small grooves we could from the ice and spent the night there, suspended with our feet stuffed into our rucksacks. We shivered silently in our individual tribulations, too far apart to pass food or drink. We popped Valium and stared into the storm-basted ribbon of sky that tacked the western horizon.

My feet were cold all night. They ached all day. I led up and left into a system of snow-clogged chimneys that left me, after several hundred feet of climbing, studying a conundrum. Above, the main chimney narrowed to a slot 3 feet wide and was blocked by an enormous chockstone. Both sides of the passage were coated with thick rime ice, white and warted as the Elephant Man's butt. I dumped my pack and bridged out tenuously. My mind wandered, taking me back to Boulder...the corner of Broadway and Pearl, to be exact. Hmmm. Bookstores and French bread, coeds and foreign cars, and—ah, yes—the "wall" on the campus of C.U. crawling with punks carrying chalk bags, so close to the center of it all, dude, you could touch it. I thought of being warm again, and about dying. I looked down and saw myself tumbling tip over tail forever, the rope streaming like a purple-and-blue contrail, no longer flirting with space but flying at last, oh yeah.

For lack of anything else to do, I nudged up, shoulders and knees, to beneath the stone at the very back of the depression and thrust my ax up into the snow gathered behind it. Pressure, rest; effort, release. An hour later I was standing above the hole I'd chopped, fixing the ropes to a cluster of ice screws and runners. I shouted down to the others to come up. I thought I heard a voice, two shouts, perhaps more, then silence again. After a while the rope went taut with the weight of a climber. I touched the gray ice and wondered: how long? We were on the Whale's Tail, riding the very back of the beast.

The night was horrid and everlasting. I was utterly spent and passed the evening lapsing in and out of groggy soliloquies about how I had to rest, man, curl up in bed somewhere warm, turn on a tap and get water, rest these weary, cold, cold arms. We sat huddled in our separate miseries and dreamed our lonely panaceas, hardly speaking, dressed in wool and nylon and feathers. My fingers pulsed, and each throb brought excruciating pains behind fingernails as white and hard as porcelain. We leaned off the edge of our serac and shat hanging from a rope, our turds dropping soundlessly into the impossible abyss.

In the morning it was still snowing. Gentle waves of spindrift hissed down the face in filmy avalanches; so we stayed put and arranged the bivouac platforms. They lacked the gaiety of the cave—they were not so warm or nearly so bright—but they were an improvement on sitting out in the wind and cold with that dark space below and the distance above eating out our eyes.

We dined on freeze-dried shrimp Creole and drank lukewarm, urine-colored tea that tasted like shrimp Creole. Food and drink came, and I took it like communion. Abrams shared my platform, maintaining his complex, pontific silence. I heard Metilkja and Hamish talking quietly from time to time, but their words lacked animation or joy.

We were in deep. Very, very deep.

The snow continued and grew heavier. The spindrift slides came episodically, great waves of frigid surf breaking over us and surging into the void, where, a day earlier, and we might have joined it, tumbling and spinning earthward like paper. We packed without comment in the morning. We left behind the rock climbing gear, a stove, the platforms, and some of the food. The hell with it: There was no going back down that way now, anyhow.

We divided into two teams again: Hamish ~~~ ~ ~ ~ ~

~~~ ~ ~~~~~ ~~

~ ~~~~ ~~

~~~~ ~ ~~~~. ~~

... ~ imagine any course of action other than what we were doing. Simply plod and hope. Storm-shrouded silhouettes, we climbed in egocentric removal from one another, companions in nothing more than the movement of the rope. We were shadows caught in random highlight against the whited-out sky. There was no sense of progress, no feeling of getting anywhere. Just the unabated impulse to go on.

In the murk of sunset we gathered on a small, uneven ledge and crouched leg to leg as Metilkja passed around sausage and cookies. We dug into our packs after headlamps and sweets. Without shelter it seemed pointless to try to bivouac in the open at such an altitude. So in our independent pools of light we continued our long crawl, waiting and climbing, waiting and climbing.

The storm, of course, got worse. We were climbing upward into the nastiness of it. The wind came in violent gusts. The temperature dropped. The snow stung our cheeks and walrus-snot icicles hung from our mustaches. I went into long lapses of memory wherein I could not recall if I had been climbing or standing still. I huddled deeper within myself seeking warmth and coherence and would increasingly return to reality uncertain of what mountain I was on or with whom.

I began to hear Abrams.

At first I thought nothing of the voice. I have no idea how long I listened to it before it broke upon me that I was hearing an external sound. It was more the sporadic wail of the storm itself than of a man yelling. It was, I thought, some shrieking in my own mind. And then, clearly, I would hear it again. A shout, a sentence. I could never make out the words, but I became convinced that it *was* a voice. And in time it occurred to me that the voice was the Major's.

That it did not stop.

That he was crazy. Mad as the moon. A *sennin.*

___

And that I was on this mountain with him, being led by him, happy about it. Hell, even I was laughing. It got so every time I heard that lunatic howl I'd grin as wide as a cat on crampons. The chaos of the storm reduced the revelation of our insanity to scale: who'd have been there but crazy people, anyway? Why go on peg-footing and stiff-lip-ping as if it all made sense in the first place? I loved it! I, too, felt like howling, but I couldn't find the air the Major could.

At the base of a 60-foot runnel of ice, the angle increased to near-vertical. I caught up with Metilkja standing roped in to a gathering of ice screws. Above us, Abrams was wailing and shouting, angry and laugh-ing. Two hundred and twenty volts of illuminated madness in that wind-bitten gloom. The stoic and dour Croat was grinning, too. We stood there smiling at each other until the screaming stopped and it was Metilkja's turn to climb. I flicked off my headlamp to save batteries and thought of Lucy. She was right, goddamnit. The Buddhists were right, too, and hell, so was the beggar in the alley for that matter. Only mad-men and tantric Mansons up here, embracing their flaky *chods,* ice-men *sennins* and their mountain Masta. It was just the right place for them.

We reached the bottom of the summit ice flutings sometime after midnight. Maybe later. I remember finding Hamish hanging from all kinds of webbing and ice gear and plastered with rime.

"Major's gone up, laddies," he said slowly. "'Fraid me hands 'ave aboot had it. Lost me fookin' mitts down there when we poot on the torches." He was trying to grin. He looked spent and sheepish, letting the rope run through hands jelled into rubbery spoons. He had his parka hood up now, but all the hours without a hat seemed to have had their effect. Metilkja took off his pack and dug into it for some spare socks to cover Hamish's hands. I took over the belay, watching Hamish as I let out the line. He seemed calm, happy, a little guilty, perhaps, b...

and Hamish, and soon Metilkja shouted and started climbing. We moved faster for a time. The snow stopped and the wind released us. I pulled hard, hand over hand, up the rope and turned a great, pillow-shaped cornice to reach the others clustered on the southwest ridge. The clouds below carpeted the valleys in every direction. The still-dark sky behind us shared its diamond stars with the pallid yellow blot of dawn. The Major stood in the saddle, ice ax in his hands, a serpentine black-and-beige rope hanging loose from his rucksack like the severed head of a Hydra. His voice was as cracked and scratched as an old recording.

"This is it, boys!" he shouted. "Here you go! She's up there, not 500 feet, by God, and we're as good as there! Fancy foot you, O'Brien, eh? It's ours, all right, and no wind, no snow to stop us now! Not when we've come halfway around the world to put our footprints up there, I tell you. The hardest wall in the world?" He laughed, pointing the spike of his ax at the heavens. "Don't let me hear that talk again. Not in front of boys like these! Come along, then, Frazier! Another few hundred feet and you can spit in the face of the God that froze your hands, man, scuff your boots on His horrible face, if you've a mind to, eh?"

His wild hair sprang horizontally as a gust of wind carried off his woolen balaclava. The vapors danced up the wall like steam to reach for the mother-of-pearl clouds obscuring the sullen sky. The Major roared with laughter at the enormous cosmic illusion of futility in which the mountain wished us to believe. Hamish was enraptured, his eyes glazed. Metilkja was harder to read: He went about his business neither awed nor annoyed. Myself, I grinned like a mouseketeer for Abrams. His madness had fueled our upward determination, but getting down was going to take a different frame of mind and I knew my best chance was with the Yugoslav. Hamish was weakening; Abrams was a whirlwind, a chimera. Only Metilkja had the feel of substance.

Metllkja and I lifted Hamish to his feet and the four of us set out. The angle was easier, and we used our axes like canes. We hiked heads down into a burgeoning gale and rested on our knees. Again I fell behind the others and had only the comfort of their footprints and the Major's occasional shout until the mists parted and I saw them standing together 20 feet in front of me.

On the summit.

Abrams was hatless and howling. Hamish crouched with his frozen hands cupped in front of him as if he were holding snowballs. Metilkja stood beside him, looking away to the east. We danced staccato footsteps, buffeted by the suddenly ferocious wind. After only a few moments Metilkja looked over to me and shouted, "Down! Now!" He pointed with his ice ax in the opposite direction from which we'd come. He spoke as if we were the only ones there. Neither Hamish nor the Major paid him the least notice.

"There is no harder wall, no harder ice, no higher point upon this mountain, lads! Tea in hell, I tell you!" the Major shouted.

⌐‾

"Down! Now!" Metilkja screamed and began to stagger off into the full blast of the wind. I gave a sharp tug on the rope connecting us.

"What about them?" I yelled, pointing at Hamish and the Major. Hamish was staring straight up into heaven as the Major babbled his crazy sermon on the mount. Babes in Toyland.

Metilkja looked at me, his haggard, black eyes as hard as glass. His glance shifted for a moment to our teammates and then came back to mine. The message was clear and I understood. He turned and worked his way down, and I waited for the rope to run out before following him. I looked at the Major and Hamish as if they were apparitions. I felt nothing for them at all. In fact, I felt nothing about anything until the rope pulled tight and I took my first step d̲ ̲ ̲ ̲ ̲ ̲ ̲ ̲ ̲

. . . .

had fought hard to get up, and now the mountain seemed to want to hold us there. The gale inflated our wind suits and pressed its hands against our chests. The cold was piercing and terrible. My face burned. Inside a thousand dollars worth of high-tech nylon, plastic, leather, and rubber I felt the cold carve through me. I did not turn and look back for the others. I closed them out of my thoughts and concentrated instead on my own wooden steps. There were no voices now: the storm shrieked louder than Abrams's feeble hoots. It gave us back the proportion of our real achievement. We hadn't "conquered" the mountain any more than a rat conquers the ocean by hiding in a ship's bilge. We'd skittered across the summit and now crept wretchedly away from any protracted confrontation with the Himalaya's true adolescent savagery. We were running away on frozen feet, less victors than survivors.

The hours were fused with snow. We reached a serac and stood in its lee to rest. My knees ached and my legs felt cold to the bone. I kept my mind off my feet. I had no idea whatsoever of where we were or where we were headed. We stood panting, our eyes interlocked. Metilkja looked withered and gaunt, awful. He motioned with his head to something behind me. Abrams came out of the storm, still crisp as a Yorkshire birder; Hamish staggered along after him.

"We'll be done within an hour, lads," the old man cheered. "We head down this ridge till we find the upper valley glacier. I looked this over last year. One man, by God! Happy me, boys, happy me! She'll not hold us off now, will she, eh? We're too close to it now!" he barked, clenching one fist and holding it up to the sky. "By Judas, don't anyone talk to me about blasphemy! Why, I'd piss up the wind if I had a mind to. This mountain is *mine*, I tell you! Send down her storm and snow; I'll shove it up spout and stand this ice while I will!" Then, lowering his arm, his eyes on fire, he seemed to speak directly to me. "Heaven and hell by the short hairs! You'll tell them that for me, won't you? Tell them it was *mine!*"

Metilkja closed his eyes and for an instant dropped his head. When he looked back up, his face was full of the old sobriety and purposefulness. He raised his compass and studied it. I touched Hamish's arm and he looked at me. His cheeks were white, his eyes sunken back a thousand synapses from the horrible truths of the tactile world. I wanted to cry. Instead, I smiled and patted his shoulder.

"See you down there," I shouted, and he nodded his head. I walked away, knowing I would never see him again.

The rope drew me down into a well of storm. I thought about dying once more, about falling, about sitting down. I thought about heat and hallucinated a room full of stuffed chairs and couches with a stone fireplace and brandy glasses on a long table spread with a linen cloth and the dirty dishes of a sumptuous meal. Metilkja was standing in the corner of the room in his wretched, wind-torn, and rime-sheeted climbing suit. He was wiping away the ice from the headlamp he had been wearing since the night before. I turned on my own light and followed him down through the gloomy penumbra beyond the banquet and into the shelter of a crevasse wall. Just beyond, the ice fell away into an abysmal pit of hurricane updrafts and utter blackness.

Metilkja dropped his pack and pulled out a bandolier of ice screws. Nine in all. I had another six. I groped to fathom our behavior. The madman had said the ridge would bring us to the glacier and the glacier to the valley. But here? And how far down? And into this storm?

Metilkja suffered none of my neurotic ambivalence. He understood function much better than I. He knew that the doing was the important part and that the outcome would either reward or penalize our boldness. One acted out of strength without hesitation or consorting with hope. One suffered the consequences to the extent he was capable of influencing them. Everything else was either magic or religion. Metilkja threaded the rope through a carabiner and

.... it through my braking device. I tilted backward and slipped down into the maw of the awful night.

Rappel followed rappel. The cold devoured us, and the wind snapped our sleeves and leggings so hard the material parted. My feet were lost, I knew that. I could feel nothing below my boot tops. I waited out my turns in an aura of torpor. No thought or feeling aroused me except to clip into the rope and slide down to where Metilkja would be waiting, his eyes always searching. During those silent, piercing, somber, shattering, wind-buffeted meetings, our faces were lit by the dim light of each other's headlamps like Welsh miners, and our silence was the only alternative to the storm.

I knew I was barely hanging on, slowing Metilkja down. I tried to meet his glances with my own strong gaze, but I knew he must be aware of my growing incapacity to think or move. I held tight to the ropes after he was down to keep him from pulling them through the anchor, stranding me.

And rappel followed rappel.

After so many that I had lost count, I found myself clipped to a set of ice screws, watching the flickering yellow light of Metilkja's headlamp disappear into the murk, when an enormous block of ice grazed the névé just above me and plunged on into the darkness, down the line of ropes. I was so frightened, so dazed, that I simply swung from my runner, cringing, my eyes closed for what seemed like fifteen minutes. The ropes were free when I lifted them; the stance below was empty when I arrived. Metilkja was not there. No screw or bollard protruded from the wall. No Croatian eyes. Just the night and the storm, the roaring black. I hung onto the ropes waiting for him. I poked around in the snow at my feet if I had missed a ledge. I swung left and right in small pendulums and called for him.

There was nothing but some crampon marks scraped in the ice.

I screamed his name, but my pathetic yap barely reached my own ears.

Perhaps he had begun down climbing, I thought. Yes! That had to be it! The climbing was easy for him. We were going too slow by rappelling; so he had abandoned me and simply begun down climbing. He had seen the same shadows in my eyes as I had seen in Hamish's: the confusion, the dependence I had on him.

I screamed until I couldn't breathe. I collapsed against the ropes, gasping and hyperventilating. Live, I told myself, live, you stupid fucker! You will *do* this thing. He's either dead or left you. They're all dead, but I will not die here, hanging on this wall, running away from this mountain. I slapped my arms to make the blood circulate and took an ice screw off my harness. I will do this thing and I will live. "I will live," I shouted, and pulled down on the ropes.

With two screws left I touched the glacier. I huddled in the protection of a small bergschrund and took off my pack. I crawled into my bivouac sack and sleeping bag. Among other things in my pack I found some sausage and two candy bars, along with an extra pair of mittens. My headlamp faded to dull orange. In its last light I found Metilkja's compass lying in the snow beside me.

I awoke at first light. It was overcast and snowing lightly, but the wind had stilled. I felt rested, weak but alert. I packed just the sleeping bag and a few odds and ends, then cut the rope in two and coiled half of

it around my shoulders. Everything else I left to the haunting and op-
pressive silence.

I lost all concept of time. I followed the compass easterly with no
notion of how far I'd come, how many crevasses I'd jumped or circled,
no idea of how far I had to go. I f . . .

. . . . stumbled pa-
thetically, incompetently. I heard voices—singing, whispers, sighs—but
saw nothing. No one. Just the enormous, hopeless white. I was exhausted
by midmorning, traveling on slowly evolving sets of rules: walk 200 paces
and rest, 200 paces and rest again. I lost count and rested. I lied and
rested. I quit counting and rested. I came to a huge pressure ride, traversing around its south side, I found what looked like the trough a person
might make in fresh snow. It was too blown over with spindrift to find
boot prints, but I followed its vague, undulating course, squinting to
pick out the subtle gradations of white.

I saw the Major from 50 feet away. I felt a remarkable absence of
surprise. The color of his clothing against the blank canvas of snow and
sky was sensational. He was sitting up against his pack. His skin was
translucent. His eyes were open and his hands were tucked underneath
the armpits of his open parka as if he had just stopped to warm himself.
He was still hatless, his hair moving slightly in the ground-level breeze.
The black-and-beige rope was crisscrossed over his chest and shoulders-
in a guide's coil. One end had been cut. I stopped in front of him. I knew
he was dead; yet it would not have surprised me if his eyes had moved
and his face had turned up. Death had not taken him; he had simply
exhausted life, worn it out.

Snow clung to the hairs of his face, and his trousers clapped in the
wind. He continued staring back at the mountain, beckoning me to turn

around, but there was nothing back there for me. Not anymore. There was nothing, to say. I lifted Metilkja's compass and continued on my azimuth.

When it became dark, I used the adze of my ax to dig out a niche between two ice boulders. I emptied what little remained inside my pack onto the snow, crawled into my sleeping bag again, and pulled the pack over my feet and up to my waist. In a small stuff sack I found a tube of lip balm. I tried to eat it and immediately threw it back up, speckling the snow with bright blood. After a time I dozed. During the night the snow changed to rain.

The air was warm and sodden when I awoke. My sleeping bag was drenched, but the rain had also washed away the snow around me, and for the first time I realized that I was no longer on the glacier. I was sitting between stones, not blocks of ice. I was on the moraine. Dirt and earth were below me. I left everything and started walking.

My feet were horrible. I began falling over everything, lying for a long time before I could rise. And then, finally, I simply couldn't get any higher than my knees. That was okay. I was prepared for it. The change came neither as a shock nor as a disappointment. Just new rules for the game. I crawled for a while, the toes of my boots dragging in the gravel and leaving twin ruts behind me like those of a tiny ox cart. I struggled through a shallow stream of icy, fast-moving meltwater and reached a large boulder on the opposite side, where I lay back and rested. I tore off bits of my wind suit and used the strips to tie my mittens to my knees.

The rain was lighter, a fine Seattle mist. Through breaks in the clouds I could look up to splashes of green on the south-facing slopes of the valley. I noted this arrangement without elation or impatience. I was anticipating nothing. I felt no excitement.

I knew that I was off the mountain and that I would live—that, if necessary, I could crawl to the trail between Kahli La and the Dutch camp and from there crawl down to the yak-herders' hut. If the Sherpas had given up on us and left, then I knew, too, that I could keep crawling…over Shipton Col, past Sedua, to Khandbari, to Kathmandu, and all the way back to Boulder. It was no folly; I knew I could succeed in this *chod*.

So I progressed, staggering a few steps on dead feet and then collapsing to basic elbows and knees, shreds of my blue wind suit clinging to the ends of willow twigs. I left blood on the first grass that I

.....g time, breathing slowly, letting the rain wash my face, and gazing up at the mountain through elliptical gaps in the clouds. It seemed as pristine and aloof to me as it had in Abrams's photographs.

Untouched. Unmoved. Unknowable.

~

Tears ran down my cheeks. I laughed. I laughed and I cried at the same time, gasping and falling over on my side, helium-headed and sick. Just me…of all the heartbeats and dreams, of all the struggle and obsession, I alone remained, more an abstraction than an alpinist, dumb as the last, great, silent *thump* at the end of the universe. I was all that was left. I cried and I laughed and I knew nothing. Only the mud and brush and pebbles.

And it was there that the Dutch expedition, returning with our Sherpas from the futile search for their lost son, found me, another soul orphaned by dreams.

ACKNOWLEDGMENTS

"Chalk" was previously published in *Appalachia* Vol. XLV. No. 1 (Sum-

previously published in *Climbing* No. 75 (October, 1979); "Poontanga" was previously published in *Ascent* No. 3 (1976); "Built On Rock" was previously published in *Mountain* No. 85 (May, 1982); "Bird" was previously published in *Climbing* No. 185 (September, 1998), under the title "The Bird"; "Cannon Mountain Breakdown" was previously published in *Mountain Gazette* No. 59 (Fall, 1977); "Mountain of Magic, Valley of Marvels" was previously published in *Mountain Gazette* No. 23 (Summer, 1974); "Leviathan" was previously published in *Ascent* No. 4 (1980).

Other titles you may enjoy from The Mountaineers Books:

A LIFE ON THE EDGE: Memoirs of Everest & Beyond, Jim Whittaker
The autobiography of the first North American to summit Mount Everest. Whittaker's account highlights the major events in his career including the creation of REI, an intimate friendship with the Kennedys, expeditions on K2 and Everest, and personal stories of friends and family.

GHOSTS OF EVEREST: The Search for Mallory & Irvine, Jochen Hemmleb, Larry A. Johnson, Eric R. Simonson
Members of the team who found Mallory's body on May 1, 1999, give the exclusive story of what they discovered on Everest and answer questions to the most enduring mystery in exploration history: Did Mallory and Irvine make it to the top? And, if they did, what happened to them?

THE BEST OF ROCK & ICE: An Anthology, Dougland MacDonald, editor
For more than 20 years, *Rock & Ice* magazine has published excellent writing from the world's best climbers. Now, for the first time, *Rock & Ice* editor Dougland MacDonald has gathered together a collection of the magazine's best essays.

DARK SHADOWS FALLING, Joe Simpson
In a narrative that is certain to challenge readers and inspire debate, Simpson examines the rise of guided climbing, media spin on climbing accidents, and incidents involving poor treatment of Sherpas.

THE TOTEM POLE: And a Whole New Adventure, Paul Pritchard
The award-winning firsthand chronicle of Paul Pritchard's physical and emotional battle to recovery after a life-threatening head injury. He weaves together accounts of earlier climbs, his accident on Tasmania's Totem Pole, his changed relationships with friends and family, and his triumphant rehabilitation.

SUMMIT FEVER, Andrew Greig
When poet Andrew Greig was asked by Scottish climbing legend Mal Duff to join his ascent of the Mustagh Tower in the Himalaya, he had a poor head for heights and no climbing experience whatsoever. The result is this unique book, enjoyed by climbers and literary critics for its refreshing candor and wit.

STORIES OFF THE WALL, John Roskelley
From his teenage climbing days to his twenty years in the Himalaya, Roskelley writes bluntly and honestly about his most significant influences on and off the mountain. A story of personal growth from one of the leading American mountaineers of his generation.

MIXED EMOTIONS, Greg Child
The famous climber writes about his mixed feelings about climbing—the loss of friends, the thrill of achievement, and the soul-shattering moments of risk and survival; but it is precisely these experiences that compel him to write and to continue climbing.